BLACK AMERICA

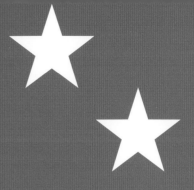

BLACK AMERICA

Kehinde Andrews, Dr. Peniel E. Joseph,
Erica Armstrong Dunbar

BLACK AMERICA

Used under license. All rights reserved. This version
published by Fox Chapel Publishing Company, Inc.,
903 Square Street, Mount Joy, PA 17552.

For more information about the Future plc group, go to
http://www.futureplc.com.

ISBN 978-1-4971-0397-9

Library of Congress Cataloging-in-Publication Data

To learn more about the other great books from Fox Chapel
Publishing, or to find a retailer near you, call toll-free
800-457-9112 or visit us at www.FoxChapelPublishing.com.

We are always looking for talented authors.
To submit an idea, please send a brief inquiry to
acquisitions@foxchapelpublishing.com.

Printed in China
First printing

Part of the
ALL ABOUT HISTORY
bookazine series

INTRODUCTION

The African-American story is undeniably one of
heartache, pain, and struggle. However, it's also one
filled with resilience, creativity, innovation, and hope.
In Black America we aim to tell that story through
a timeline of the historic events, significant figures,
and cultural milestones that have come to represent
the Black American experience. Over the pages you'll
discover fascinating features on the events of the Civil
Rights Movement, the birth of soul music, African-
American involvement in World War II, how Black
athletes broke down racial barriers in US sport, the
origins of the BLM movement, and much more.

CONTENTS

8

8 FIRST BLACK AMERICANS

10 AMERICA'S CENTURIES OF SLAVERY

14 PHILLIS WHEATLEY

16 UNCLE TOM'S CABIN

18 NAT TURNER'S REBELLION

22 FREDERICK DOUGLASS: SLAVE TO STATESMAN

28 HARRIET TUBMAN: SLAVE, SPY, SUFFRAGETTE

36 AMERICAN CIVIL WAR

38 EMANCIPATION

40 BLACK COWBOYS

42 RECONSTRUCTION

44 JIM CROW LAWS

46 WASHINGTON & DU BOIS: THE POWER OF EDUCATION

50 THE NAACP IS FOUNDED

52 HARLEM RENAISSANCE

56 TULSA RACE MASSACRE

58 JESSE OWENS

60 THE BLACK EXPERIENCE IN WORLD WAR II

64

74

64 LEVELING THE PLAYING FIELD IN US SPORT

70 BROWN V BOARD OF EDUCATION

72 EMMETT TILL

74 ROSA PARKS: TIRED OF GIVING IN

78 LITTLE ROCK NINE

80 AMERICA GOT SOUL

86 SIT-INS AND FREEDOM RIDES

88 BIRMINGHAM CAMPAIGN

80

60

136

92 'I HAVE A DREAM'

100 BIRMINGHAM CHURCH BOMBING

102 MISSISSIPPI MURDERS

104 CIVIL RIGHTS ACT

106 SELMA TO MONTGOMERY MARCH

110 MALCOLM VS MARTIN

120 THE BLACK PANTHERS

126 BLACK POWER SALUTE

110

128 I KNOW WHY THE CAGED BIRD SINGS

130 JIMI HENDRIX AT WOODSTOCK

132 SHIRLEY CHISHOLM RUNS FOR PRESIDENT

134 RUMBLE IN THE JUNGLE

136 RISE OF HIP HOP

142 THE OPRAH WINFREY SHOW DEBUTS

144 RODNEY KING AND THE LA RIOTS

146 BARACK OBAMA: FIRST BLACK PRESIDENT

150 BLM: THE NEW CIVIL RIGHTS MOVEMENT

156 THE GEORGE FLOYD PROTESTS

158 KAMALA HARRIS

146

150

A woodcut showing enslaved Africans being introduced to Jamestown, Virginia, in the 1600s

A census from Virginia shows the first documented African woman, Angela, to arrive at the colony

FIRST BLACK AMERICANS

The story of Black America goes back 500 years, when the first captured Africans were brought to the New World; the original members of a burgeoning, resilient community

The first known Africans to set foot on North American soil were a group of enslaved people brought by the Spanish to present-day South Carolina from Santo Domingo (Haiti) in 1526 to found a new colony. They were brought as part of the expeditions that followed Christopher Columbus's first voyage, but following a struggle for control, they set fire to the houses and fled to freedom among nearby Native Americans. The Spanish too quickly fled back to Santo Domingo and the precedent had been set for a long history of resistance and rebellion against oppression.

The first surviving Africans in English America were the "20 and odd Negroes," Angolans originally captured by the Portuguese, who came to Jamestown, Virginia, on the famous voyage of 1619 as indentured servants. In fact, most early Africans in the Americas were not actually enslaved; they were servants made to work unpaid for seven years to pay off their passage and upkeep. They were treated brutally but eventually were free to go with a release payment and provision to start a new life. Indentureship was not lifelong or hereditary like slavery. Thus, in the early days, a lively free Black population owned farms, grew wealthy, and made major contributions to the young new nation.

Forging a life for these early African Americans was tough, but there is evidence of surviving, flourishing African art, music, religious and culinary practices, trade and financial systems, and languages. They came with knowledge of agricultural techniques, medicine and technology that fundamentally shaped America and the crops and food staples still in place today. Many were urban Angolans who were highly educated and cosmopolitan. They demanded freedom, shaping and contributing to American ideals.

The first instance of lifetime slavery wasn't recorded until 1640, when an indentured servant, John Punch, was sentenced to lifetime servitude for running away. From the 1660s, racial, inherited slavery became more widespread, and in 1699, Virginia deported all free Blacks, with those remaining enslaved. Though Black Americans were an important free community that contributed to the beginnings of the US, as racism evolved, things began to change. Between 1690 and 1710, the population of Africans in British colonies tripled from 16,700 to 44,900 through the slave trade. Just before the Revolutionary War, 22 percent of the American population was Black, and mostly held in bondage.

The importation of Black Africans was seen as the ideal solution to an emerging labor problem in North America. White settlers and Native Americans were rapidly dying, so Africans who were used to a similar climate and seemingly resistant to many of the diseases killing the indigenous population were brought in

AMERICA'S CENTURIES OF SLAVERY

America was founded on the principle of liberty and justice for all, but it wasn't the land of the free for everybody

America didn't invent slavery, but it embraced it with horrible enthusiasm. Slaves were the backbone of the American economy. Between 1790 and 1860 the harvesting of cotton in the Southern states grew from a thousand tons a year to a million, with slaves the crucial labor force needed to bring in those crops. In 1790 there were half a million slaves in the South. There were four million by 1860. The system was backed by legislation, the courts, the military, and the government. The importation of slaves actually became illegal in 1808, but the law went unenforced, meaning that hundreds of thousands of slaves continued to be brought into the country, usually from Central and Western Africa. The system was so entrenched that only the Civil War could bring it to an end.

Slaves had a low life expectancy and were treated more like cattle than human beings; they were sold at auctions, where their physical attributes and talents were talked up as their most marketable qualities. Slave owners would often break up families, selling husbands or wives, or their children. This was often a deliberate policy to subdue the slaves' spirits – after all, a slave without a family was thought to have less will to resist. There were also sometimes economic reasons: at one point there was such a surplus of slave labor in the Upper South that a forced migration of more than a million slaves to the Deep South was implemented. Through all of this, slaves held on to their humanity. Torn from their families, they formed deep kinships with their companions on the plantations. Music, dancing, art, and religion all remained important

> **Slaves in Kentucky in the 1860s were valued between $40 to $400 each. Strong males in their 20s were highly prized**

– although the latter could be used against the slaves. Black preachers were also sometimes employed to preach in ways that kept the slaves in line.

Whippings and other brutal punishments were not only widespread but normal. Slave revolts were unusual since they were swiftly put down with military force. Escape was more common, although risky. Successful runaways made new lives in Canada, Mexico, or the North, but getting caught in the process of escape meant getting torn apart by dogs, or shot. The Fugitive Slave Act was passed in 1850 to make it easier for slave owners to reclaim their 'property' south of the border in Mexico, and there were laws to dissuade White people from giving aid to escaped slaves. Poor, uneducated White people were employed as overseers of Black labor, entrenching White racism in the South for decades to come.

Unsurprisingly there were uprisings, although most were swiftly crushed. One of the most famous was led by Nat Turner on August 21, 1831. Turner and his band of brothers were ultimately unsuccessful, and security in the South became even tighter as a result of their rebellion. But the voices of abolitionists were getting louder. In 1853, John Brown (a White man) hatched a plan to seize the federal arsenal at Harpers Ferry, Virginia, and spark a slave revolt throughout the South. Local militia, plus hundreds of marines under the command of General Robert E. Lee, put down the insurgency (Brown was hanged), but it was clear that the issue was far from concluded. Still, as late as 1857 the Supreme Court ruled that Dred Scott could not sue for his freedom because he was property and not legally a person.

Robert E. Lee, the commander of the defeated Confederate States Army

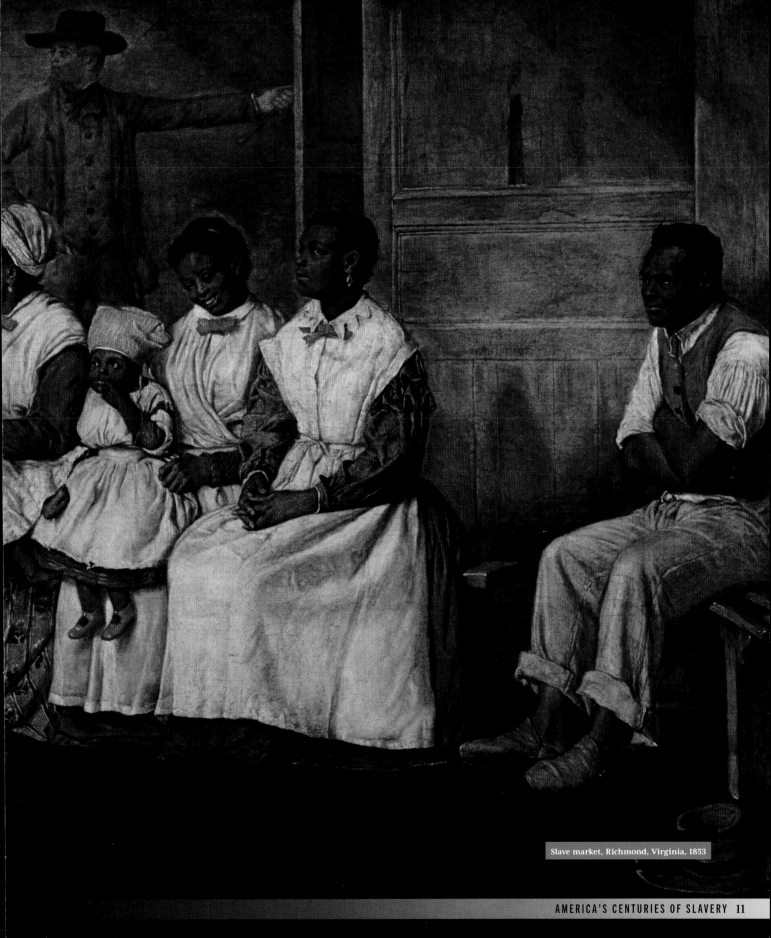

Slave market, Richmond, Virginia, 1853

Union Army general Ulysses S. Grant became president in 1869 and worked to protect the civil rights of former slaves

Slaves were the most valuable asset of the American economy, worth roughly $3 billion in 1860

All of the above took place under the presidency of Andrew Jackson. Abraham Lincoln replaced him in 1860, with discomfort about slavery part of his platform (though he wasn't strictly abolitionist). The secession from the Union of 11 pro-slavery Confederate states reliant on slave labor for the plantation system took place the same year. Lincoln began leaning politically slightly further to the left thanks to the continuing pressure of abolitionists.

Congress passed the Emancipation Proclamation, declaring slaves on all Confederate territory immediately free, in 1862, although the North was hardly a utopia of equality: citizens were still allowed to own slaves as long as they were loyal to the United States. Lincoln argued passionately about the humanitarian wrongness of slavery (although he was careful not to advocate any sort of social or political equality between White and Black). By the summer of 1864, buoyed by the Emancipation Proclamation, anti-slavery petitioners had sent 400,000 signatures to Congress demanding slavery be abolished. The Senate and the House of Representatives signed off on the Thirteenth Amendment to the US Constitution. Slavery was legally over.

While the government could legislate against slavery, however, it could hardly legislate against racism. With the Civil War now regarded to a great extent as one of Black liberation, the resentment of White people drafted to fight in it became dangerously volatile (especially since the draftees were usually poor – Whites with money could buy their way out of fighting). There were draft riots, in which cities were overrun with anti-Black violence. But the African Americans in the South now found themselves with unexpected power, since the Confederacy, perversely, needed them to fight the Union. It could either free its slaves, enlist them in its army and use them to fight in the war – thereby negating the point of much of the conflict – or it could refuse and watch its enslaved workforce down tools and defect to the Union Army. Congress granted equal pay to Black and White soldiers in April 1864. A year later, with the Confederate troops depleted and demoralized, the war was finally over. Lee surrendered to Grant.

Despite the new rights of freed African Americans to vote, be educated, and serve politically, however, White American society, especially in the South, remained aggressively opposed to equal rights for Black people. President Andrew Johnson, who took office after Lincoln's assassination, was firmly on the side of the Whites on these issues, refusing legislation leaning towards racial equality. Slavery may have been over, and Black children attending school, but former slaves found themselves living and

Nat Turner and companions depicted in 1831

NAT TURNER'S SLAVE REBELLION

Nat Turner lived his entire life in Southampton County, Virginia. Intelligent and religiously devout, he could read and write at an early age and, by his twenties, he was preaching services to his fellow slaves. He became known locally as 'The Prophet' for that reason, and because of the spiritual visions he claimed to have. One such vision in 1828, when Turner was 28, inspired him to begin planning a violent uprising, which finally took place in August 1831. Turner interpreted a solar eclipse on the 13th of the month as a sign from God for the slaves to begin the fight back against their oppression.

Having banded together a force of about 70 men, Turner began traveling from house to house in Southampton County, freeing slaves and killing their White 'masters'. The murder was indiscriminate, including women and children, and Turner and his rebels were responsible for at least 60 deaths before they were stopped, finally overwhelmed by a White militia with more than double the manpower of the insurrectionists. The uprising had lasted two days.

Over 50 Black men and women were executed in the aftermath on charges of murder, conspiracy, and treason. Turner himself was hanged on November 11, and his corpse flayed, decapitated, and dismembered. The following year in Virginia, it became illegal for slaves to be educated, or to hold religious meetings in the absence of a White minister.

On February 24, 2007, Virginia became the first state to acknowledge and publicly apologize for its history of slavery

Slaves on the plantation of the Confederate general Thomas F. Drayton, South Carolina, 1862

"WHITE AMERICAN SOCIETY REMAINED AGGRESSIVELY OPPOSED TO EQUAL RIGHTS"

working on the same plantations, unable, both financially and legally, to buy or rent their own land, and forced to work under strict labor contracts with prison sentences the punishment for breaking them. These were the Black Codes that formed the antecedents of the 'Jim Crow' segregationist laws of the 20th century.

Black votes played a huge part in the election of President Ulysses S. Grant in 1869, and with Johnson out of the picture, some societal progress was made, with equality laws passed and constitutional amendments put forward.

But whenever the cause of African-American rights advanced, there was White resistance to meet it. Racist groups like the Ku Klux Klan sprang up to terrorize Black people and keep them oppressed, and as those groups gained more and more members, politicians desperate for votes were forced to pander to them. The African-American blacksmith Charles Caldwell shot a White attacker in self-defense and was acquitted of murder at the subsequent trial. He was the first Black man ever to kill a White man in Mississippi and go free. Not long afterwards, however, he was murdered by a White gang. The White South was going to continue to make its own justice, regardless of laws that suggested otherwise.

THE INCREDIBLE HARRIET TUBMAN

Harriet Tubman was born into slavery in 1822 in Maryland. She was violently mistreated throughout her young life – at one point sustaining a serious head wound from a thrown metal weight, the after-effects of which remained with her for the rest of her life. But that life was a long and eventful one.

Aged 27, she escaped the plantation she was indentured on, making use of the 'Underground Railroad', a network of safe houses and abolitionist activists dedicated to helping slaves gain their freedom. She subsequently became prolifically active in the Railroad herself, undertaking daring missions back into Maryland to help rescue other slaves. She was so successful at it that the abolitionist William Lloyd Garrison dubbed her 'Moses'.

Tubman was a devout Christian who absolutely abhorred violence, but nevertheless later became a 'General' in John Brown's (ultimately unsuccessful)

Harriet Tubman, photographed in 1900

insurrectionist movement. When the Civil War broke out in 1861, she identified the Unionist cause as the one most likely to bring about an end to slavery, and worked as a scout and a spy in Confederate territory, helping to free slaves in their hundreds.

Well into her seventies, she became active in the fight for women's suffrage. She died from pneumonia, aged 91, in 1913, in a rest home named in her honor.

PHILLIS WHEATLEY

Phillis Wheatley was the first African-American woman to publish a book of poetry, and is widely considered fundamental to the genre of African-American literature

There is no record of what the little girl that would later become Phillis Wheatley was doing on the day she was stolen from her home, somewhere in West Africa, around 1760. After surviving the horrifying journey across the Atlantic, at seven years old, she was enslaved by John Wheatley and his wife, Susanna, in Boston, Massachusetts. They named her after the ship she was transported on, and after deciding that she was more intelligent than the rest of those they enslaved, they separated and educated her. Phillis excelled in Latin and Greek, and began writing poetry.

In 1770, the publication of Phillis's poetic tribute to an evangelist preacher gained her some notoriety. However, many White academics found it difficult to believe that an enslaved African woman could possibly be writing poetry, so in 1772, she was 'examined' by a group of White men who eventually wrote a letter to confirm her authorship.

Accompanied by her captor's son, Nathaniel Wheatley, Phillis traveled to London in 1773, aged 20. There, she published a collection called *Poems on Various Subjects, Religious and Moral*, which was well received. Phillis's poetry rarely engaged with her identity as an enslaved Black person – an exception being *On Being Brought from Africa to America*, which went on to become one of her most well-known works.

Phillis cut her trip short and returned to Boston when Susanna Wheatley became ill. A month later, she was freed. After Susanna's death in 1774, Phillis became more vocal about her views on slavery. In a published letter to a Native American minister, she described enslavers as "modern Egyptians," drawing parallels between Africans and the Hebrews of the Old Testament. In 1778, Phillis married John Peters, a free Black man from Boston. The couple had three children together, none surviving infancy. At some point after 1780, John was prosecuted for debt and the couple fled Boston. On returning, he was incarcerated and Phillis got work as a scrubwoman in a boardhouse. She died due to complications from childbirth in December 1784, aged 31.

Following his wife's death, John kept trying to publish her second book. Some of the poems from this volume were later recovered and released in collections. Regardless, her work was frequently cited by abolitionists, and used to promote equal education.

A statue of Phillis Wheatley is part of the Boston Women's Memorial in Commonwealth Avenue Mall, Boston

P O E M S

O N

VARIOUS SUBJECTS,

RELIGIOUS AND MORAL

BY

PHILLIS WHEATLEY,

NEGRO SERVANT to Mr. JOHN WHEATLEY,
of BOSTON, in N__ E_____

L O N___

Printed for A. BELL, Boo____
Meſſrs. COX and BERR___

MDC___

Arch.ᵈ Bell,

WHEATLEY, of BOSTON.

UNCLE TOM'S CABIN

Harriet Beecher Stowe published over 30 books, but is known around the world for one in particular: the bestselling anti-enslavement novel *Uncle Tom's Cabin*, published in 1852

The book opens on the Shelby plantation, Kentucky (in around 1850), introducing two enslaved people – Uncle Tom and a boy called Harry – about to be sold. The story then splits into two plot lines, one focusing on Uncle Tom and the other on Eliza, Harry's mother.

While being transported to an auction by boat, Tom saves the life of a young White girl called Eva, and is purchased by her father. Later, a violent White enslaver called Simon Legree becomes Tom's new captor after Eva and her father both die. Legree finds any excuse he can to terrorize Tom, determined to crush his faith in God. Throughout it all, Tom's character remains dignified, noble, and resolute in his faith. Meanwhile, Eliza and Harry make a dramatic escape and eventually reunite with Harry's father and journey north to Canada.

Stowe's inspiration came from several places, including her immersion in abolitionist writings, her visit to a Kentucky plantation as a young adult, and her Christian faith (she sometimes claimed it was "the result of a vision from God"). She also searched anti-enslavement newspapers for first-hand accounts and invited others to send her information.

Uncle Tom's Cabin was an instant bestseller. In the US, it sold 10,000 copies in its first week and 300,000 in the first year. It was the bestselling novel of the 19th century.

Stowe became a leading voice in the anti-slavery movement, despite her use of derogatory language and offensive racial stereotypes in *Uncle Tom's Cabin* that exposed her many misconceptions about Black people. People from the 19th century up to the present day have debated whether Stowe had the right to speak for enslaved African people, acknowledging that her whiteness meant she had a wider reach than a Black author would have had at the time.

In the build-up to the American Civil War, Stowe's novel dramatically shifted public opinion about the enslavement of African people. During the 20th century, however, it was heavily criticized by many Black writers, including James Baldwin in his 1949 essay "Everybody's Protest Novel." The term 'Uncle Tom' has since become an insult, used to describe a Black person filled with self-hatred who is somehow complicit with white supremacy. The development of the insult was likely inspired by the early theatrical adaptations of the novel, which often distorted Uncle Tom and changed the ending to make more comfortable viewing for White audiences of the time.

This illustration from an early-20th century edition of Uncle Tom's Cabin, published by Frederick Warne, London, shows Tom reading his Bible to women in the hut

This quarter-plate daguerreotype of Harriet Beecher Stowe was probably made around the time of the publication of Uncle Tom's Cabin (1852)

SLAVE UPRISING: THE NAT TURNER REBELLION

Often attributed to its leader, Nat Turner, the Southampton Rebellion was a natural consequence of the brutal Southern slave system

n 1831, a group of enslaved people in Virginia launched a 36-hour rampage that left almost 60 White people dead. Although the White establishment was desperate to paint the incident as an anomalous plot organized by a bloodthirsty barbarian, the reality spoke for itself. It was the natural consequence of the brutal system of slavery so deeply threaded into the veins of Southern antebellum society.

At the turn of the 19th century, the invention of the cotton gin had completely transformed the South. The American cotton industry, centered in the Deep South, exploded, becoming the country's leading export as it fought its way towards international trading supremacy. With profits soaring, so too did demand for slaves, and when the international slave trade was abolished in 1808, Upper South states like Virginia gained a stranglehold over the country's domestic slave market.

By 1820, two-fifths of Virginia's one million population were enslaved people, with 1.5 million more scattered across the South. Slaves were the legal property of their owners, who enforced strict control over how they lived, dishing out cruel punishments for those who broke the rules. For the enslaved, simply holding social meetings and church services were great acts of rebellion.

While slave owners and overseers were responsible for supervising slaves during the day, Virginia's 101,488 militia members took care of the night patrols. One Southampton County resident, Allen Crawford, recalled: "Patrollers would whip you if they caught you without a pass."

White slave owners used systematic brutality to keep Black slaves in perpetual terror. One escapee, Julian Wright, had a chain clamped around her leg so tightly it became infected, stripping all the flesh from the bone. When a Virginian slave, Lucy, could not work the fields because she was in labor, her overseer whipped her so severely she later died – her daughter born with lash marks on her back. Another, Fannie Berry, recalled how after being severely whipped, a fellow slave remarked, "Fannie, I don' had my las' whippin'. I gwine to God," before killing herself.

As a natural reaction to this oppression, many enslaved people developed their own system of evasion – keeping their meetings secret while sending lookouts to track patrols and, if need be, lead them into dead ends or strategically placed brambles. One group kept a pile of hot ash and coals ready during meetings, hurling it when the patrol arrived.

In the 1820s, the Deep South's cotton supply grew so large the global price dropped by 55 percent. The resultant depression clogged up the domestic slave market, leaving Virginia with a massive slave population. In 1829, Virginia governor John Floyd warned the legislature about the "spirit of dissatisfaction and insubordination" among the country's slaves. While this received little attention, a minor media frenzy accompanied the acquittal of a Black man, Jasper Ellis, accused of "promoting an insurrection of the slaves."

This "spirit of dissatisfaction" was only amplified when the Virginia Constitutional

Convention of 1829-30 maintained a commitment to slavery. Ironically, the delegate Charles Ingersoll, who argued that "no one man comes in the world with a mark on him to designate him as possessing superior rights to any other man" was a staunch anti-abolitionist.

Although the country's leading abolitionists met at the Negro Conventions of 1830 and 1831 to propose creating a college for Black people, the Virginia legislature only further suppressed and disenfranchised slaves. It banned free Black people from congregating for the purposes of education, marrying Whites, or living with slaves, and sold all Black criminals into slavery.

It was in this climate, amidst the hot and sticky swamps and forests of Southampton, torn between endless brutality and fleeting promise, that Nat Turner fomented his violent rebellion. Born a Southampton slave in 1800, rebellion ran in Turner's blood: his father had run away, successfully escaping all the way to Liberia. Turner began having religious experiences as a young boy and, having learned to read and write, grew up believing himself to be a prophet

In the early 19th century the Deep South's cotton industry exploded, creating an unprecedented demand for enslaved workers

interpreting coded messages from God in visions and signs in nature. These visions culminated in "a loud noise in the heavens", a solar eclipse and an atmospheric phenomenon that, by August 1831, convinced him that he must rise up in violent revolt.

On August 21, after a night spent dining on a stolen pig, Turner led a group of followers to his master's house, where they butchered the entire family with hatchets – even a sleeping infant. During the following day-and-a-half the rebels moved from plantation to plantation, freeing slaves, taking weapons and murdering every White person in their path. At their peak the rebels numbered around 50, killing almost 60 people before being dispersed by the local militia 36 hours into their rampage. While most of his accomplices were arrested and executed, Turner remained on the run.

Although the rebellion lasted less than two days, it sent a tidal wave of terror and hysteria across the South. Plantations were abandoned as owners whisked their families away to hideouts, anticipating further carnage. Rumors spread of further insurrections, such as fictitious stories of maids caught plotting to kill children, Black men caught with huge arsenals of guns, and Turner sightings across the country. When a second rebellion in neighboring North Carolina involving 25 slaves was betrayed by an African-American freedman, the paranoia reached frenzied heights. In the Virginia town of Petersburg, when a report of a 500-strong slave rebellion was proved to be a false alarm, an English bookseller remarked that Black people should be emancipated. He was stripped, lashed, and chased out of town.

Amidst the panic and hysteria, White volunteers rode across the South, torturing, burning, and murdering many African Americans they came across. Newspapers ran stories on prolific killers, one of whom boasted of lynching 15 Black people alone. In Georgia, slaves were tied to trees en masse and hacked to death. One enslaved person who had saved his master from the rebels was gunned down by his owner for refusing to help track them down.

After six weeks, Turner was discovered by chance in Dismal Swamp by a hunter. The last rebel to be caught, he was interviewed in jail by a wealthy Southampton lawyer and slave owner, Thomas Gray. The subsequent essay, "The Confessions of Nat Turner", was used as evidence against him during his trial. Less than a fortnight after his capture he was found guilty and hanged before a large crowd. His corpse

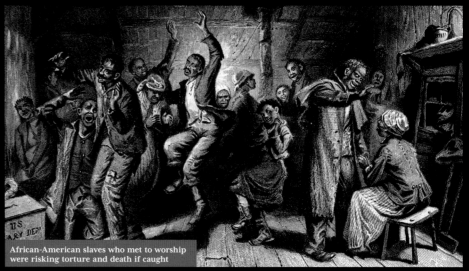

African-American slaves who met to worship were risking torture and death if caught

was skinned and his flesh turned into souvenirs and grease, his bones handed out as keepsakes.

Though Turner was dead, his belief that other slaves would rise up to claim their rightful freedom was shared by the White establishment, who desperately sought to contain White fear and mitigate slaves' expectations. Virginia's governor John Floyd delivered a paranoid address to the legislature, stressing the need to silence Black preachers and shut down freedom of movement. Even though free African Americans had nothing to do with the revolt, the governor saw them as the driving force behind the emerging abolition movement.

Turner's revolt brought the issue of slavery to the forefront, and before long the Virginia legislature was inundated with petitions and requests ranging from the emancipation of slaves to the deportation of free Black people to Africa. On January 25, 1832, after fierce debate, the legislature's special committee concluded

"FOR SLAVES, SIMPLY HOLDING SOCIAL MEETINGS AND CHURCH SERVICES CONSTITUTED GREAT ACTS OF REBELLION"

The violent events of August 1831 shocked Virginia's White establishment to its core, forcing it to re-evaluate its commitment to slavery

A HISTORY OF AMERICAN SLAVE REVOLTS

The Southampton Rebellion is often considered the most 'successful' revolt, but it wasn't the first or even the largest

While some historians have identified records of more than 300 slave revolts in the US alone, the country's first all-Black rebellion took place in Virginia in 1687 with the Westmoreland Slave Plot. Half-a-century later, in 1739, a slave named Jemmy led 100 Angolan slaves on a killing spree across the Stono River region towards St. Augustine, Florida, where they would be free under Spanish law. They fought for a week before being suppressed by the English, inspiring a series of subsequent revolts.

Two years later, when a series of fires broke out across New York and Long Island, it was blamed on a joint slave-Catholic conspiracy, sparking off a witch-hunt. Despite little evidence, up to 40 enslaved people were hanged or burned at the stake, alongside four Whites. Many more were exiled.

In 1791 the slaves of Saint-Domingue, the world's most profitable slave colony, rose up in revolt against their French colonial masters. Thirteen years later they emerged victorious, founding the independent nation of Haiti. Among those who were inspired by the Haitian Revolution was a literate enslaved blacksmith known today as Gabriel Prosser who, in 1800, planned to raise 1,000 slaves in revolt beneath a banner of 'Death or Liberty'. But he was betrayed and executed alongside 25 Black men.

Just 11 years later another slave inspired by the Haitian Revolution, Charles Deslondes, organized a rebellion along Louisiana's German Coast with the aim of capturing New Orleans. After swelling to roughly 125 men, the rebels were only defeated after two days of bitter fighting when they ran out of ammunition. After the battle, 100 enslaved people were executed and their severed heads placed along the road to New Orleans.

On July 3, 1859, White abolitionist John Brown and his two sons led a raid on Harpers Ferry, Virginia, hoping to instigate a slave rebellion. Despite successfully liberating several slaves, they were eventually put down by local militia and Brown was hanged for treason.

The Southampton Rebellion was one of many slave revolts inspired by the successful Haitian slave revolution

that while most of its members believed slavery was evil, none were willing to pay the price of abolishing it. The committee chairman, William Brodnax, lamented the result but expressed faith that slavery would someday be eradicated gradually.

With emancipation off the cards and the bill to deport Black people to Africa postponed indefinitely by the Senate, Virginia and its neighboring states introduced a series of laws designed to further suppress Black people's rights. These included banning African Americans from meeting in groups after 10 p.m., preaching without a licence, immigrating, owning arms, attending their own religious services, learning to read, selling food or tobacco, and buying alcoholic spirits.

While the Southampton Rebellion did not inspire the wider revolution Turner had hoped it would, it did force Southern slave states to recognize that slavery was an evil that must one day be abolished. It was not Turner's Rebellion, but a reflex reaction to the systemized barbarity of slavery. The event left a gaping wound in the legitimacy of slavery that would be torn wide open just decades later as the country erupted into Civil War, marking the end of American slavery and the beginning of a new chapter in the fight for civil liberty.

During the six weeks Nat Turner remained on the run, the South was swept up in violent anti-Black hysteria

FREDERICK DOUGLASS: SLAVE TO STATESMAN

Discover the remarkable rise of an agitator, reformer, orator, writer, and artist

Frederick Bailey was most likely born in February 1818 (although there are no records to prove the exact date) in his grandmother's slave cabin in Talbot County, Maryland. He was probably mixed race: African, Native American, and European, as it's likely that his father was also his master. His mother was sent away to another plantation when he was a baby, and he saw her only a handful of times in the dark of night when she would walk 12 miles to see him. She died when he was seven.

Frederick was moved around and loaned out to different families and households throughout his childhood. He spent time on plantations and in the city of Baltimore, a place he described as much more benevolent towards enslaved people, where they had more freedom and better treatment than on plantations. Indeed, Baltimore was one of the most bustling harbor cities in America, a meeting place of people and ideas of all kinds from all around the world; a place in which dreams and visions of freedom could easily be fostered.

One mistress, Sophia Auld, took a great interest in the 12 year old, teaching him the alphabet. But her husband Hugh greatly disapproved of teaching slaves to read and write, believing it would equip them to access ideas and aspirations beyond their station. It would make them rebellious. Eventually, Sophia came to agree with Hugh's disapproval and herself believe that teaching slaves to read was wrong. She ceased her lessons and hid his reading materials, snatching newspapers and books from the enslaved boy's hands when he was caught with them.

But Frederick was shrewd and continued to find ways to learn, trading bread with street children for reading lessons. He learned to buy knowledge and words from a young age. The more he read, the more he gained the language and tools to question and condemn slavery, developing his sense of Black identity and personhood for himself. When he was hired back out to a plantation owned by William Freeland, Frederick set up a secret Sunday school where around 40 slaves would gather and learn to read the New Testament.

Douglass was taught to read by his master's wife, Sophia Auld, but her husband convinced her to stop as he opposed teaching slaves literacy

This picture shows Douglass fleeing barefoot from two mounted pursuers with dogs

Surrounding plantation owners gradually came to know of these clandestine meetings and one day descended on the group armed with stones and clubs, permanently dispersing the school.

Not long after, Frederick was sent to work for Edward Covey, a poor farmer with a dreadful reputation as a 'slave breaker'. He was sent to be broken, to have his rebellious spirit crushed and be transformed into a docile, obedient worker. He faced frequent whippings, and at just 16 he resolved to fight back, physically asserting his strength over Covey. Frederick tried to escape once but failed.

That was before he met Anna Murray in 1837. Anna was a free Black woman in Baltimore who was five years older than him. The pair quickly fell in love and she encouraged him continuously to escape and find freedom, helping him to realize that freedom was truly within his grasp. The following year, in 1838, aged 20, Frederick made his break from the shackles of slavery.

He made the passage from slave state to free

Anna Murray-Douglass, Douglass's first wife of 44 years, was known as a patient, loyal, and caring woman

state in under 24 hours, boarding northbound trains, ferries, and steamboats until he made it to Philadelphia in Pennsylvania, then a Quaker city with a strong anti-slavery sentiment. He then traveled to New York disguised in a sailor's uniform. He faced many close shaves, even catching the eye of a worker whom he knew, and who mercifully remained silent about seeing him. On setting foot in the north, Frederick was a new man, master of his own destiny. He was free to decide the direction of his own life for the first time, a thrilling and overwhelming prospect. Murray joined him up north, where they were quickly married and could now decide on their own name.

They tried out Johnson, but eventually decided on Douglass. Settling in abolitionist stronghold towns in Massachusetts, they played active roles in a church community populated by many prominent former slaves, including Sojourner Truth and later Harriet Tubman.

By 1839 Douglass was a licensed preacher, a role in which he honed his speaking skills.

He was also an active attendee of abolitionist meetings and developed strong friendships with campaigners like William Lloyd Garrison, who wrote the weekly newspaper *The Liberator*. Aged 23, Douglass gave his first anti-slavery speech at the Massachusetts Anti-Slavery Society Convention in Nantucket, and began touring across the country with fellow abolitionists. His rapid ascent from slave to celebrity took place over little more than one year.

As one of the few men to have escaped slavery with a willingness and ability to be so eloquent about his experiences, Douglass became a living embodiment of the impacts of slavery and an image of Black stature and intellect; a vision of what African-American people could become. He was used by White abolitionists to oppose general stereotypes of African Americans as ignorant or lazy. In some ways, Douglass became like a zoo animal on display, a success story trophy, and he knew it. This strained his relationships with some other major abolitionists, like Garrison. Nevertheless, Douglass also recognized the power of challenging and reshaping harmful caricatures of Black people and began to take hold of and manipulate his own representation in speeches, writing, and images.

Douglass spent two years touring Ireland and Britain between 1845 and 1847, lecturing and meeting with the last remaining abolitionists from Britain's abolition movement of the early 19th century, such as Thomas Clarkson. It was during this time that Douglass finally gained legal freedom and protection from recapture, with English acquaintances raising the funds to officially buy his freedom from his master Thomas Auld. The public endorsement Douglass received from influential figures in Europe only increased his credibility in the States. He returned with £500 donated by English supporters and used it to set up his first abolitionist newspaper, *The North Star*. Alongside this, he and his wife were active in the Underground Railroad, taking over 400 escaped slaves into their home, offering them rest and safety on their journey to freedom.

Douglass was an advocate for dialogue and alliances across ideological divides. Notably, he was a supporter of women's suffrage campaigns and attended many events in favor of the cause, such as the

> **"DOUGLASS BECAME AN EXAMPLE, A LIVING EMBODIMENT OF THE IMPACTS OF SLAVERY, AND AN IMAGE OF BLACK STATURE AND INTELLECT"**

Seneca Falls Convention, at which he was the only African American present. Though he faced a backlash for his contribution, it was only after Douglass's speech that a resolution was passed in favor of female suffrage, indicating his power as an orator. But his interaction with the cause was controversial, because not everyone was in favor of women's rights. Many believed African-American freedom, equality, and suffrage was the far more pressing and urgent issue, and that Douglass's endorsement only gave more power to White female voters, who would vote against Black people's interests.

But Douglass was more astute than this. Indeed, Richard Bradbury argues that, bolstered by his tours through Ireland and Britain, he connected the struggle against slavery with many other issues: poverty in newly industrialised London, Irish famine and Home Rule, and women's rights. In his later years as a statesman, Douglass even engaged with Caribbean and Latin

Douglass appealing to President Lincoln and his cabinet to enlist Black men

A deep split in the abolitionist movement reveals the complexity of Douglass's vision and ideology

Historian David Blight refers to Frederick Douglass as one of the most critical readers, as well as speakers and writers, of the time. This is in reference to Douglass's radical reading of the US Constitution and the conflict it caused between himself and fellow abolitionist William Lloyd Garrison. Garrison believed that the US Constitution was an exclusive, elitist text that did not hold a place for the abolition of slavery or provide a legal or moral precedent for abolition. In this sense, the United States was constitutionally, fundamentally, intrinsically pro-slavery, a bleak thought for abolitionists to accept. In demonstration of his disgust at this, Garrison burned a copy of the Constitution.

At first, Douglass agreed with Garrison's reasoning. However, he later became influenced by Lysander Spooner's publication of *The Unconstitutionality of Slavery* in 1846. This bolstered Douglass's idea that the Constitution did not support slavery, and slavery was not enshrined in the very idea of America's nationhood. The Constitution could and should be utilized as a tool to justify abolishing slavery, and was a document with good intentions that had been corrupted and misused. This caused Douglass and Garrison to break apart their partnership in 1847. It was the greatest notable split in the American abolition movement.

Douglass's understanding of how slavery was or was not bound up with the concept of the nation is seen by many historians as significant for its sophistication. Later, at the dawn of the Civil War, Douglass held great appreciation for Abraham Lincoln's insight that slavery could only be abolished if the nation – the Union – was violently fought over and won on the premise of being a free, non-slaveholding country, creating a fresh start. Douglass was both radical and conservative, imagining the violent upheaval of his world to make space for a new reality, but in which the tools of the current world could be invaluable.

He knew that America could only exist free of slavery if it underwent a major transformation, yet he also campaigned fervently against the popular idea of 'colonization', which suggested that slaves should be freed and sent to the Caribbean or back to Africa. Douglass saw that African Americans had to have a stake in building this new nation and deserved to fight and defend their freedom, and he convinced Lincoln to allow African Americans to serve in the Union Army. Though the US denied the humanity of slaves, Douglass did not seek to deny the United States as his nation, nor see it as necessary to remove Black people in order to achieve freedom. Instead, Black people must themselves have a hand in building it. He was American and believed that America could be fundamentally redesigned to include and accept him.

A PHOTOGRAPHIC PIONEER

Photography was a major part of Frederick Douglass's belief system and his efforts to defeat slavery and racism

At a time of great social change in the 19th century, photography was quickly growing as a new art form. With the invention of daguerreotypes, it was increasingly cheap and accessible, and Douglass saw it as a democratic medium that could serve the needs of the people. He considered that whereas politicians could lie, peddling false images and caricatures of slaves to justify slavery's continuation, the camera would tell the truth. Nuanced, serious, sophisticated images of Black people portrayed as human beings rather than property could challenge negative images, particularly blackface and minstrelsy.

Douglass was the most photographed American of the 19th century (even more than Abraham Lincoln), a remarkable record for a Black man and ex-slave. Around 160 images of him have been found, taken over many years. He stared directly into the camera, confronting the viewer, and never smiled. Typically, the sitter would be asked to stare softly into the distance or look beyond the camera, and to smile. But Douglass's stare holds a challenge to be taken seriously – he did not want to present himself as a smiling, happy, obedient slave. Simultaneously, he played into other trends recognizable to the eyes of White viewers as dignified, educated, wealthy, and accomplished; his formal dress and swept-back hair took on the attributes of a classical hero.

His portraits were reproduced as lithographs and engravings and distributed to promote his talks. His use of photography was subversive and highly political, reflecting his sophisticated political philosophy, his understanding of how public opinion was formed and influenced by the media, and his belief in the social power of art.

A rare photograph of Douglass with his second wife, Helen Pitts Douglass

American ideas about multiculturalism and democracy in challenging White supremacy. And he was interested in issues affecting Native Americans and recent immigrants. He was American, through and through, but he also looked beyond the nation that had enslaved him and legally rejected him as a fellow man and citizen, towards the international stage. This gave him a space to construct and consider what he stood for and enter into dialogue with those in a like-minded pursuit of change. This global, cross-struggle outlook has helped to make Douglass such a modern, sympathetic figure, with communities across the world claiming him for their own. He created a greater sense of a united class of downtrodden people who could together overthrow their common oppressor through coordinated efforts.

One of Douglass's chief arguments, as illustrated in his famous *What to the Slave is the Fourth of July?* speech of 1852, was the importance of education in improving the lives and opportunities for African Americans. He was an early advocate of school desegregation, building upon his early experiences teaching at his Sunday school as a slave. He was also a deeply religious and spiritual man and believed that Christianity did not endorse slavery. Douglass chose to abstain from alcohol, tobacco and other 'corrupting' substances to keep his body 'pure'. Like many involved in struggles against oppression who took divine inspiration, from Thomas Paine to Nat Turner to Elizabeth Cady Stanton, he saw himself as a prophet heeding God's will.

Douglass published three versions of his life story, in 1845, 1855 and 1881 (with a revised edition in 1892). Each autobiography, written at different stages of his life, have different tones, aims and ideological outlooks. By the time of the American Civil War in 1861, Douglass was one of the most famous Black men in America. He was both an ardent supporter, and honest critic, of Abraham Lincoln and his approach to ending slavery. Later, during the Reconstruction era Douglass went on to receive several political appointments, such as becoming the President of the Freedman's Savings Bank.

During a violent period of backlash against newly emancipated slaves, and the rise of the Ku Klux Klan, Douglass supported Ulysses S. Grant in his 1868 presidential campaign to combat segregation and violence. Grant sent Douglass on a mission to the West Indies

This contemporary print places Douglass as a highly distinguished and central figure of both racial politics and American politics at large

A statue of Douglass in the US Capitol's Emancipation Hall in Washington, D.C.

and Haiti, leading him to work with the US government on issues related to the Caribbean and its potential. Grant wanted to see if Santo Domingo could be a good sight for the US to annex as an additional state to relieve racial tensions by providing African Americans with their own state. Later, in 1889, President Harrison appointed him as the US minister resident and consul-general to Haiti, and the chargé d'affaires to Santo Domingo. So popular and influential did Douglass become in the top echelons of American politics that he became the first African American to be nominated for vice president of the United States (though without his knowledge or approval) in 1872.

This latter part of Douglass's life was turbulent. Though he was highly revered and favored, there were, of course, critics and he was often in danger. His home was at one point burned down in an arson attack, causing him to move to Washington, D.C. with his family. A disagreement with radical abolitionists

"HE CREATED A GREATER SENSE OF A UNITED CLASS OF DOWNTRODDEN PEOPLE WHO COULD TOGETHER OVERTHROW THEIR COMMON OPPRESSOR THROUGH COORDINATED EFFORTS"

caused him to flee into exile abroad. His family life also became a focus of gossip and scandal: he had two affairs with White women while his wife Anna was alive. She died in 1880, and Douglass remarried two years later to a White suffragist and abolitionist 20 years his junior, Helen Pitts.

His affairs and controversial second marriage tainted Douglass's reputation. Indeed, later accounts written by his children (Douglass had five), indicate that the real saint may have been their mother, who remained Douglass's most ardent supporter, protecting his name and retaining the dignity and respectability required of women at the time, despite her husband's affairs and absences. Shockingly, despite Douglass being one of America's most revered writers and intellectuals, his first wife remained illiterate all her life.

Douglass continued touring and traveling, speaking and campaigning into his final days – literally to his very last moments. After receiving a standing ovation for a speech on women's suffrage in 1895, the 77-year-old Douglass collapsed with a heart attack. Thousands passed by his coffin to pay their respects, and he continues to be honored by countless statues, remembrances, and plaques across the globe. He is remembered for his understanding that agitation, education, work, and reform were the crucial areas in which change could transform the lives of African Americans, and America as a whole.

© Alamy / Getty Images

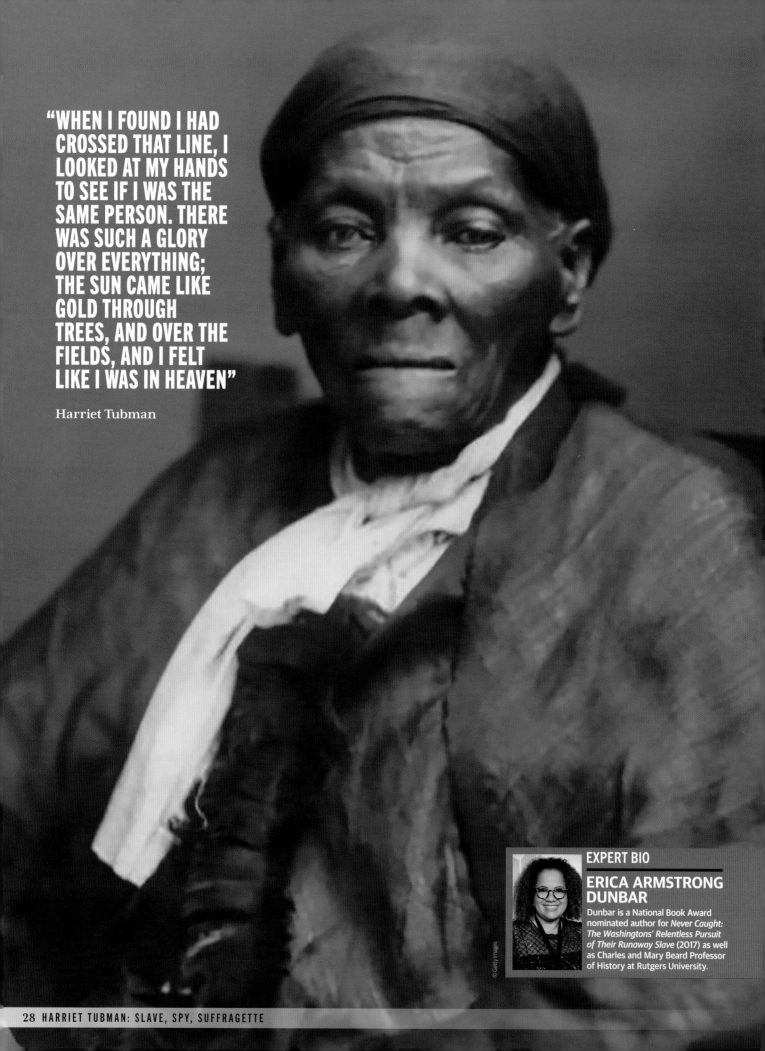

"WHEN I FOUND I HAD CROSSED THAT LINE, I LOOKED AT MY HANDS TO SEE IF I WAS THE SAME PERSON. THERE WAS SUCH A GLORY OVER EVERYTHING; THE SUN CAME LIKE GOLD THROUGH TREES, AND OVER THE FIELDS, AND I FELT LIKE I WAS IN HEAVEN"

Harriet Tubman

EXPERT BIO

ERICA ARMSTRONG DUNBAR

Dunbar is a National Book Award nominated author for *Never Caught: The Washingtons' Relentless Pursuit of Their Runaway Slave* (2017) as well as Charles and Mary Beard Professor of History at Rutgers University.

HARRIET TUBMAN: SLAVE, SPY, SUFFRAGETTE

Erica Armstrong Dunbar tells us how Harriet Tubman freed herself from bondage, went on to save others, and then fought oppression in all its forms for the rest of her life

Any single one of the milestones that Harriet Tubman achieved in her life would be enough to cement someone's place in the history books. She freed herself from slavery and went on to free others working on the Underground Railroad leading refugees out of the Southern slave states. She joined the Union Army as a spy, scout, and nurse and even led an expedition to free slaves during the war. She fought for women's rights to vote after the war. And while all this was happening she battled personal heartache and physical disability. It's an extraordinary and inspiring story, brilliantly retold by Erica Armstrong Dunbar in her book, *She Came to Slay*, so we sat down to talk through it all.

What were some of the formative moments in Harriet Tubman's upbringing, having been born a slave in Maryland?

I think that when we start thinking about Harriet Tubman, we have to think about her connection to her ancestors. I don't begin the book in 1822 when she was born. I begin with the connection to her maternal grandmother who was a woman named Modesty who was forced to travel the Middle Passage and arrived in the colony of Maryland.

So, when I think about where Harriet Tubman's story begins, I'd argue that it really begins in Africa and it begins with the strength of her grandmother. I think about the impression that her ancestors would have had on her, but I also think about her life as a small child on the Eastern Shore of Maryland. For Araminta (Harriet's birth name) she was introduced to a life of enslavement at the age of five, when she was removed from her mother's care. Think about a five or six-year-old, someone who does not yet have their adult teeth, to be taken from their family and forced to do very difficult labor; emptying muskrat traps, doing domestic work, caring for infants when she herself was but a child. This was Araminta's introduction to the hard labor of enslavement. And that loneliness was something that she would always remember.

Was she a born leader?

I don't know that I would say that she was a born leader. I would say that she became a leader and became a leader before her time on the Underground. I think that we see samples of this, for example when she was a 13- or 14-year-old girl. She was forced to make a decision about helping an overseer attempt to capture or subdue an enslaved man at the general store. She refused to get involved and I see this moment as a crucial moment for Araminta because she made a decision not to assist in the violence of slavery. Because of that decision, she was met with a serious consequence, which was that in this blind rage the overseer picked up a metal weight from the counter and hurled it in the direction

© Alamy

Image source: wiki/William H. Cheney

Here Tubman poses on the far left with some of her extended family, who all escaped slavery, around 1885

of the enslaved man who was attempting to run off and it hit Araminta in the head. It literally fractures her skull and she lived with the vestiges of this traumatic injury. Really, it was a traumatic brain injury, one that forced her to deal with headaches for the entirety of her life as well as these sleeping spells – that's what she called them. Perhaps today we would call them epileptic seizures. In any case, it was this moment when she stood up against slavery. I would argue that's a moment where we see the early signs of her leadership.

This injury had other effects on her life too?

We often think about the head injury as just that, an injury. But I think there are two things that we need to remember. This injury literally disabled Harriet Tubman and we don't think about her through the lens of disability, but we really should. And she managed to live with this for the entirety of her life.

But the other thing that we need to remember is that she also says that this is the moment where she becomes the closest to God, and she was a deeply spiritual and religious person for her entire life. It was this head injury that brought about these sleeping spells, and during these spells she would have visions that would prompt her on what was going to happen. They were almost premonitions.

Of course, these premonitions, these visions, helped her on the Underground. She said this later on in her life. She recounted to her biographer that she had these visions and they would tell her which way to cross a road, how to stay away from slave catchers, which bridge to cross, which one not to cross. When we step back and we think about the awesome and almost unbelievable life that she led on the Underground Railroad, one almost has to believe that there was some kind of divine intervention to allow a small woman – five feet tall – to make 13 successful trips in and out of the jaws of slavery from Maryland to the Northern States and Canada.

> **"IT WAS AT THIS MOMENT HARRIET REALLY MAKES THE DECISION THAT NO MAN IS EVER GOING TO MAKE THAT KIND OF DECISION FOR HER AGAIN"**

Tubman hired a lawyer to challenge for her freedom. Was this common?

No. An enslaved woman, who is illiterate, made the decision to hire an attorney because she understood or felt that something was amiss regarding the legal status of her family. She was able to hire herself out, pay her owner $50-60 a year and then save her own money.

One would think that you save money and you buy clothing or at least cloth to make clothing, extra food, or what have you. But she makes the decision to pay an attorney and this attorney scours the legal documents that are available and uncovers exactly what Araminta (at that point now Harriet Tubman) knew, which was that she was entitled to freedom at the age of 45 and that indeed her mother had been given that right and that it had been stripped from her. And this, of course, tells Harriet Tubman everything that she needs to know.

What did she face when she escaped in 1849?

Most people think they know the story of Tubman and her escape. She hopped on the Underground Railroad and appeared in Pennsylvania, but of course it was not that simple. Her first attempt was an aborted mission, not by her own desire, but because her brothers felt uncomfortable and wanted to return and basically dragged Harriet back to the farm. It was at this moment that Harriet really makes the decision that no man is ever going to make that kind of decision for her again. No man will control her movements. So she sets off by herself.

The fact that she sets off alone and as a woman is unique and very unlike the majority of fugitives who found their way to living in the North. The majority of them were young men, relatively healthy. They weren't charged with the responsibilities of child care and

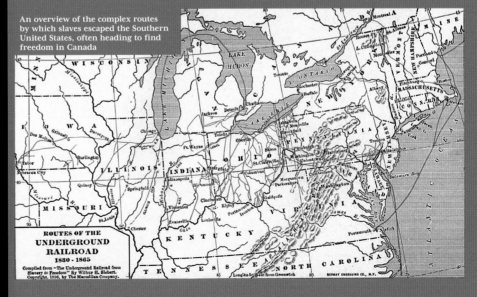

A depiction of refugees being guided by conductors on the Underground Railroad

Image source: wiki/Charles T Webber

things that kept enslaved women tethered to their farms and plantations. Now, Harriet of course did not have biological children and did not have that keeping her attached to the farm.

When she did run she used this loosely connected system of safe havens that we call the Underground Railroad. It meant that she traveled for weeks on her own, in the winter. She could not read or write, so she could not read signs or a map, let alone a compass if she had one. She was completely dependent upon the few bits of information she had from those who were willing to help her on the Underground, some of whom were free Black men and women and others who were White men and women who stood against the institution of slavery.

She hid in barns, she hid in wagons, she ate what food she could find, of which there was not much, and would travel over 100 miles pretty much by foot to reach the Pennsylvania border. We often think of this moment as Tubman reaching freedom, but in many ways that's inaccurate. It was the moment that she reached a state that no longer practiced slavery, but the federal government weighed in and she was still an enslaved person no matter where she lived, with the exception of Canada.

How did her experience inform how she then helped others achieve their freedom?

The moment that she crossed the Pennsylvania border, one would think that she would have felt immediate joy, but she actually didn't. She

WHAT WAS THE UNDERGROUND RAILROAD?

A quick explanation of emancipation efforts before the Civil War

The secret network of safe houses, roads, routes, and supply chains that helped escaping slaves make their way north, often into Canada where they could find safe haven, was known as the Underground Railroad. The route itself was not a train line, but rather named in reference to the lines that were in the early to mid-19th century helping to connect the far reaches of the expanding United States.

The network is likely to have originated with Quaker abolitionists around Philadelphia and North Carolina at the turn of the century, but was greatly expanded by the abolitionist movement as it grew. The

people who helped refugees escape were known as conductors and the stops along the way, be they people's homes, barns, or schools, were referred to as stations, safe houses, and depots, which in turn were run by stationmasters.

While in Tubman's time slavery was not practiced in the Northern US, it was still not safe for escaped slaves as they were still legally recognized as the property of slaveholders. Only reaching Canada, where slavery was outlawed completely, could escapees really find their freedom, at least until after the Civil War.

An overview of the complex routes by which slaves escaped the Southern United States, often heading to find freedom in Canada

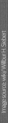

Image source: wiki/Wilbur H. Siebert

ROUTES OF THE UNDERGROUND RAILROAD 1830 - 1865

Compiled from "The Underground Railroad from Slavery to Freedom" By Wilbur H. Siebert. Copyright, 1898, by The Macmillan Company.

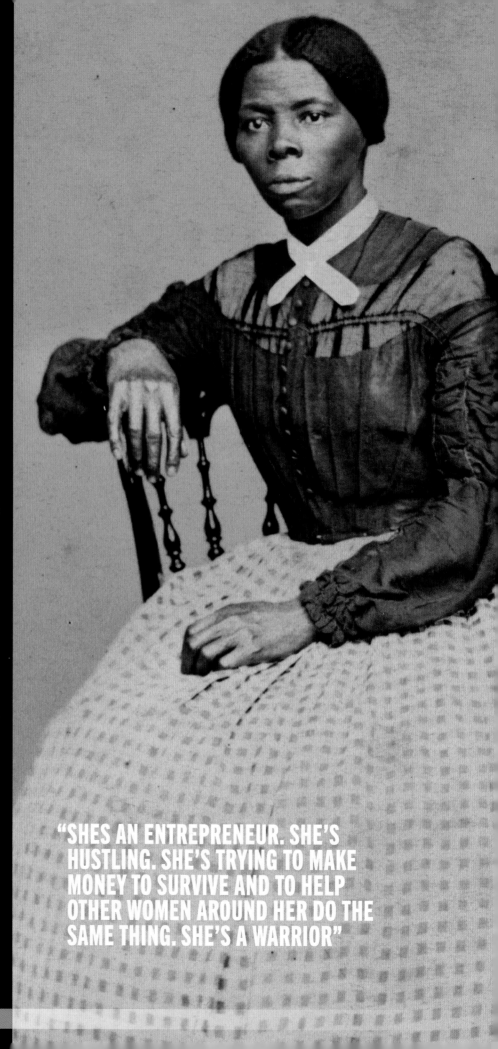

felt isolated and sad and wondered why she was in this strange land welcomed by none and that all of her family were still behind on the Eastern Shore of Maryland. It made her wonder: what does freedom mean when it sits alongside slavery? What does freedom mean when your parents or your children or your siblings are still enslaved? Almost immediately she makes the decision that she's going to go back and rescue all of them. If she could make it to Philadelphia then she would be the vessel to rescue her family and friends, so she makes this decision that her own escape and her own opportunity for freedom informs and fashions her decision to return and to help those who were closest to her.

How much danger was she in?

The risk was so very great that once again it's almost unbelievable that she elected to go back at least 13 times. There were rewards out for her capture. She returns to the Eastern Shore of Maryland, her last trip was in 1860, and so really she escapes in 1849 and for 11 years she's going back and forth, preferring to go in the winter, which was actually not the time that most fugitives attempted to escape. They usually escaped in spring and summer.

She would sometimes take the train south, which of course we sit here and say, "What? She got on a train and went south?" But yes, she did, because who is looking for fugitives on a train going back to the South? No one really. And of course she would use that, she would use the waterways, she would use wagons and foot travel. Each time she returned she was in greater danger. Each time she left she would leave with a handful of what was considered human property, so the bounty on her head grew and grew. The danger never disappeared.

How did she get involved with the Union Army?

One of the things that Harriet Tubman did frequently was make small appearances and speak to anti-slavery groups throughout New England, so she became somewhat well known, although in a very careful way, because she was still a fugitive. But in 1862 she was actually approached by the governor of Massachusetts who knew that her skills as a scout, and as someone who'd rescued over 70 people out of Maryland, could be put to good use. He convinced her to head south to Southern Carolina to serve as a scout and a spy for the Union Army.

I think it's actually incredible when we think about her heading down to Beaufort, South Carolina, in 1862. One thing to remember is that she is still technically a fugitive, and when Lincoln issues the Emancipation Proclamation, supposedly emancipating enslaved people in states that have seceded from the Union, her home state of Maryland had not seceded. She was still technically a fugitive.

"SHE'S AN ENTREPRENEUR. SHE'S HUSTLING. SHE'S TRYING TO MAKE MONEY TO SURVIVE AND TO HELP OTHER WOMEN AROUND HER DO THE SAME THING. SHE'S A WARRIOR"

While her life is full of examples of self-sacrifice and caring, Tubman could be tough and hard-nosed when she had to be, even threatening to shoot an escapee for fear they would give away Underground Railroad secrets if they backed out

TUBMAN'S ALLIES

The men and women who fought by her side

Sojourner Truth
ABOLITIONIST, WOMEN'S RIGHTS ACTIVIST

The first Black woman to win back custody of a child from a slaveholder, Truth had escaped slavery herself in 1826 and became a noted speaker for civil rights and preacher, made famous by her "Ain't I a Woman?" speech in 1851. She recruited troops for the Union Army during the war.

William Still
UNDERGROUND RAILROAD CONDUCTOR, WRITER, ACTIVIST, HISTORIAN

His record-keeping as a conductor for the Underground Railroad gives us detailed accounts of the work done by abolitionists in the region. Still personally helped fugitive slaves before the war and continued as a philanthropist afterwards.

John Brown
ABOLITIONIST

Believed the only way to end slavery was through violence, and led several armed rebellions around Kansas. He met Tubman at the Constitutional Convention (an abolitionist meeting) in Ontario, 1858. The next year he led a raid on an armory in Virginia, was caught and tried for treason.

Frances Harper
ABOLITIONIST, SUFFRAGIST, TEACHER, WRITER

Worked on the Underground Railroad, and was a public speaker for the American Anti-Slavery Society and founder of the National Association of Colored Women. She was one of the first African-American women to be a published author in the US.

Susan B. Anthony
WOMEN'S RIGHTS ACTIVIST, SUFFRAGIST, ABOLITIONIST

Put forward the women's suffrage amendment that became the Nineteenth Amendment of the Constitution. Anthony was a lifelong abolitionist, led several women's suffrage organizations and published a women's rights newspaper.

Frederick Douglass
ABOLITIONIST, WRITER, SUFFRAGIST, DIPLOMAT

Douglass escaped from slavery in Maryland and became a leading abolitionist. He wrote several books about his experiences as a slave and believed in equality between all peoples, and as such supported women's suffrage.

So here she is, a fugitive, going further south than she has ever been before, agreeing to spy and to scout. She manages to make connections with enslaved Black men and women on the ground to gather intelligence, and it's really because of her relationships in South Carolina that she's able to lead the first expedition led by a woman in the Civil War. She leads a successful expedition in which they dismantle Confederate troops and set free over 750 enslaved people. She does this while she's also serving as a nurse in the military camp hospitals. She's also creating opportunities for enslaved women to take care of themselves, taking washing in for soldiers and making food, baking pies, and these kinds of things. She's an entrepreneur. She's hustling. She's trying to make money to survive and to help other women around her do the same thing. She's a warrior.

The next stage of her life was the fight for suffrage. How did she adapt to this field?
Many of the women, White women in particular, who were involved in the fight to end slavery transitioned into or were working on securing women's rights – specifically the right for women to vote. This became intensified after the passage of the Fifteenth Amendment, which gave Black men the right to vote.

We see Harriet Tubman really working side by side with many of the White women abolitionists who had come to her rescue financially and in other ways, and stood shoulder to shoulder in the attempt to end slavery. We now see the social

movement transition to the right for women to vote. Tubman is someone who manages to walk the line well between her commitment and relationship with White women suffragists and with a new generation of young Black women suffragists who were discouraged from participating in what was seen as a heavily White woman-run movement. White Southern suffragists were unwilling to accept Black women as a part of the movement. She did the work and ultimately for her the most important thing was advancing the rights of women no matter how it came.

Was the racism of White suffragists a big issue?
The National Association of Colored Women have Harriet attend their first meeting and praise her and celebrate her. Yet, the same kind of respect and affirmation did not come from White women in the same circles. They were willing to allow Black women to participate in suffragist campaigns, however in a segregated fashion. They wanted them to march at the end of the line in their marches. For Black women that was simply unacceptable. It was quite a strain and one could argue that this strain that centered on race would be something that really plagued the women's movement throughout the 20th century.

Is there any one story about Tubman that really exemplifies her determination for you?
I think her time after the Civil War, is

> ## "I FIND IT ABSOLUTELY AMAZING THAT SHE MANAGED TO CARVE OUT A LIFE OF HER OWN AND TO MARRY AGAIN. AND TO MARRY A MAN WHO WAS 20 YEARS YOUNGER THAN HER"

© Getty Images

© Alamy

A QUEEN'S BLESSING

How did Harriet Tubman come to be buried with Queen Victoria's Jubilee Medal?

When Harriet Tubman passed away in 1913, she did so with very little money (if any), but surrounded by friends. She was buried with something rather special, however; a medal marking Queen Victoria's Diamond Jubilee in 1897. But how had she come to possess such an item?

"My understanding and that of Tubman biographers is that it was given as a gift and she was invited to the Diamond Jubilee as a guest," explains Dunbar. "She was unable to attend, but Queen Victoria wanted to make certain that she was at least recognized, so she sent her this pin."

Queen Victoria apparently also sent Tubman a silk shawl, which is now at the National Museum of African American History and Culture. But as Dunbar explains, it symbolizes more than that.

"I think it reminds us that Tubman was globally known as a leader and as a freedom fighter. It wasn't something that was simply put about on the Eastern Shore of Maryland or the South, but across the Atlantic, in England, and other places across Europe. People knew Tubman's name and I think that it's symbolic and important to think about her being buried with that marker, that medal."

SHOW ME THE TUBMANS

While her life is full of examples of self-sacrifice and caring, Tubman could be tough and hard-nosed when she had to be, even threatening to shoot an escapee for fear they would give away Underground Railroad secrets if they backed out

Tubman was expected to be replacing Andrew Jackson on the $20 bill in the US as of 2020, but the redesign has now been delayed until at least 2028

something that really marked living with the vestiges of slavery and racism. She lived for 53 years after the war's end, so living for half a century through the failures of Reconstruction, always struggling with poverty, I find it absolutely amazing that she managed to carve out a life of her own and to marry again. And to marry a man who was 20 years younger than her. There's a moment where we say, okay Harriet. I see you. Good for you! Managing to find love and companionship in the most difficult of times. I really think that her ability to pull together her family and to create lives for themselves after the Civil War and after slavery in the most destitute of financial conditions, that was amazing and often goes neglected or at least not spoken about.

The SS Harriet Tubman was a Liberty Ship launched in 1944 to aid in the war effort. Liberty Ships were cargo ships adapted from a British design that greatly improved industrial output at the time

Tubman suffered from the injuries sustained in her youth right to the end of her life. It's claimed she even had surgery without anesthesia in her old age

Guards of the 107th United States Colored Troops outside a guard house at Fort Corcoran, Virginia

A recruitment poster aims to enlist Black men to fight for the Union Army in the Civil War

A Confederate charge against Black Union soldiers at the Battle of the Crater

CIVIL WAR

The American Civil War, as the final act in a long process of the abolition of slavery and the emancipation of the enslaved, was never just fought by White Northern abolitionists

African Americans had been architects of their own liberation from the very first days of slavery, actively partaking in resistance and rebellion against the system, and particularly so during the Civil War. Indeed, many historians have found that the abolitionist movement and the winning of the Civil War could not have been possible without the agitation of the enslaved and free Black population. They defined the war by running away, escaping to Union camps where they could enlist in the Union Army. Contraband slaves (who were freed after 1863) could receive relief and protection: the Union Army decided not to enforce the Fugitive Slave Act, and thus did not send back runaway slaves to the South. Later, the Union even confiscated slaves from rebels.

Contraband camps became staples of Union encampments. They were still racially segregated and unequal, but Black soldiers successfully fought for equal pay and later military pensions. It was not just Black men, either; female contraband would work in encampments doing laundry, feeding, and clothing the soldiers. Harriet Tubman, the great conductor of the Underground Railroad, worked as a laundress and a spy for the Union Army. Approximately 200,000 Black men served in the Union Army and Navy. Meanwhile, enslaved people on plantations used the general chaos to enact greater rebellion, resist punishment, do less work, and disrupt the status quo. Others worked on plantations as Union spies, scouts, and informers.

Towards the end of the war, the Confederates became desperate and forced their remaining slaves to take up arms on the opposite side, and many enslaved fighters did what they could to sabotage their own army. The Black community across the nation did their bit to accelerate the Civil War, presenting logistical challenges for the Union and forcing them to consider the moral question of slavery, and transformed the hearts and minds of Northerners unfamiliar with the reality of slavery. African Americans were never benevolently handed the gift of freedom: they strove to create the conditions in which slavery could not survive.

EMANCIPATION

The Emancipation Proclamation redefined the course of the Civil War and set a new precedent for how the nation would be reshaped at its conclusion

When the Union Army won the Battle of Antietam in September 1862, President Abraham Lincoln knew it was now possible to issue an Emancipation Proclamation to end slavery. After great political struggle, it came into effect on January 1, 1863, in the middle of the Civil War, and celebrations abounded across the nation at the moment of liberation.

But emancipation was not just a singular, spontaneous event; it was a long, arduous, and devastating process going back at least 30 years and reaching far into the future. Nor were the impacts immediately transformative. It meant that any African American on American soil would be free, but nationwide freedom depended on a Union victory. Thus, slaves could either run away to Union land and immediately gain freedom, or through the advancement of the army into Confederate land. Between 25,000 and 75,000 slaves were immediately freed by the Proclamation, in formerly secessionist land already captured by the Union. With each success of the Union Army, more enslaved people were freed, until their final victory emancipated all remaining slaves.

The Thirteenth Amendment, ratified in 1865, set the changes in stone, so that they could not be overturned outside of the war. The Proclamation enraged Southerners and pro-slavers, who saw it as the end of the world they knew and the beginning of a violent race war. For African Americans and their allies, it was both a momentous, joyous moment, and one full of anxiety and fear over what would come next.

Lincoln was adamant that emancipation meant a totally new path for the nation, which required new measures and structures. He insisted on Reconstruction plans for the Southern states, which would help to support African Americans in building new lives from nothing, offering them "forty acres and a mule." This failed to become a reality, though, as even most Republicans were opposed to confiscating and redistributing the land of ex-slaveholders.

Reconstruction was a fraught and violent process, with many setbacks. African Americans continued their struggle for more complete freedom, as they always have. Emancipation gave them greater control and security over their families, communities, churches, and education, serving as a foundation for future struggle. Emancipation was a momentous, symbolic, legal, and moral moment that would resound across the centuries, and yet, very little actually changed for the material circumstances and safety experienced by African Americans. The signing of the document was only the beginning.

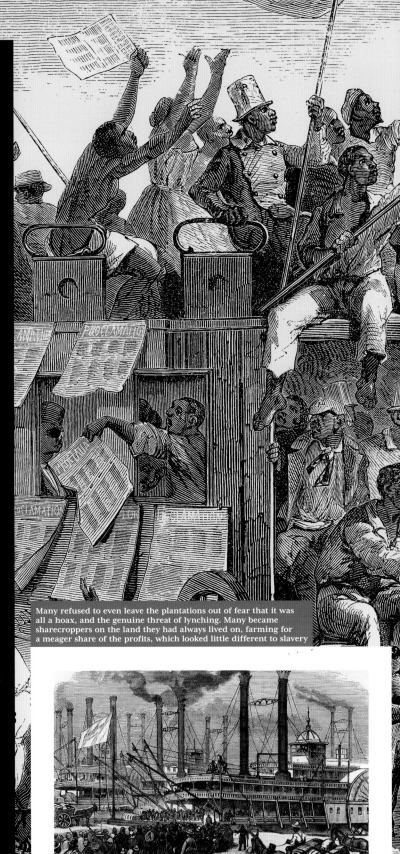

Many refused to even leave the plantations out of fear that it was all a hoax, and the genuine threat of lynching. Many became sharecroppers on the land they had always lived on, farming for a meager share of the profits, which looked little different to slavery

Emancipation Proclamation

AND HIS

Whereas On the Twenty-second day of September, in the year of our Lord one thousand eight hundred and sixty-two, a Proclamation was issued by the President of the United States, containing among other things the following, to-wit:

"That on the first day of January, in the year of our Lord one thousand eight hundred and sixty-three, all persons held as slaves within any State, or designated part of a State, the people whereof shall then be in rebellion against the United States, shall be then, thenceforward and forever free, and the executive government of the United States, including the military and naval authority thereof, will recognize and maintain the freedom of such persons, and will do no act or acts to repress such persons, or any of them, in any efforts they may make for their actual freedom.

That the executive will, on the first day of January aforesaid, by proclamation, designate the States and parts of States, if any, in which the people thereof respectively shall then be in rebellion against the United States, and the fact that any State, or the people thereof, shall on that day be in good faith represented in the Congress of the United States by members chosen thereto at elections wherein a majority of the qualified voters of such State shall have participated, shall, in the absence of strong countervailing testimony, be deemed conclusive evidence that such State and the people thereof are not then in rebellion against the United States."

Now, therefore, I, ABRAHAM LINCOLN, President of the United States, by virtue of the power in me vested as Commander-in-Chief of the Army and Navy of the United States in time of actual armed rebellion against the authority and government of the United States, and as a fit and necessary war measure for suppressing said rebellion, do, on this first day of January, in the year of our Lord one thousand eight hundred and sixty-three, and in accordance with my purpose so to do, publicly proclaim for the full period of one hundred days from the day the first above mentioned order, and designate as the States and parts of States wherein the people thereof respectively are this day in rebellion against the United States, the following, to-wit:

ARKANSAS, TEXAS, LOUISIANA (except the parishes of St. Bernard, Plaquemines, Jefferson, St. John, St. Charles, St. James, Ascension, Assumption, Terre Bonne, Lafourche, St. Mary, St. Martin, and Orleans, including the city of New Orleans), MISSISSIPPI, ALABAMA, FLORIDA, GEORGIA, SOUTH CAROLINA, NORTH CAROLINA and VIRGINIA (except the forty-eight counties designated as West Virginia, and also the counties of Berkley, Accomac, Northampton, Elizabeth City, York, Princess Ann and Norfolk, including the cities of Norfolk and Portsmouth), and which excepted parts are, for the present, left precisely as if this Proclamation were not issued.

And by virtue of the power and for the purpose aforesaid, I do order and declare that all persons held as slaves within said designated States and parts of States are and henceforward shall be free; and that the executive government of the United States, including the military and naval authorities thereof, will recognize and maintain the freedom of said persons.

And I hereby enjoin upon the people so declared to be free, to abstain from all violence, unless in necessary self-defence, and I recommend to them that in all cases, when allowed, they labor faithfully for reasonable wages.

And I further declare and make known that such persons of suitable condition, will be received into the armed service of the United States to garrison forts, positions, stations and other places, and to man vessels of all sorts in said service.

And upon this act, sincerely believed to be an act of justice, warranted by the Constitution, upon military necessity, I invoke

The Proclamation impacted the lives of 3.5 million of the four million enslaved African Americans in the US, stating that slaves in all ten secessionist states of the Confederacy would be freed

BLACK COWBOYS

Hollywood would have us believe that the cowboys of the Western frontier in the 1800s were almost always White; in reality, at least 25 percent of them were Black

In the early 1500s, the Spanish arrived in Mexico and began building ranches. The indigenous people who herded cattle on horseback were called vaqueros, from the Spanish word 'vaca', meaning cow, but in the first half of the 19th century, White Americans seeking cheap land began moving to Texas, then a Spanish territory. In order to set up and establish farms and ranches, they relied on the labor of enslaved people.

Texas joined the Confederacy in 1861. Though the Civil War hardly reached Texas, many traveled to fight. While away, ranchers depended on slaves to maintain their land and cattle. After emancipation, the ranchers hired free and highly skilled African Americans in paid roles. The term 'cowboy' was initially exclusively used to describe them – a continuation of enslavers using 'boy', a derogatory term – with White handlers generally called 'cowhands'. There were also Black cowgirls, who often used to hide their skills for fear of seeming too masculine, or disguise themselves as men so that they could join the drives.

The legendary cattle drives of the 1800s saw cowboys travel thousands of miles on horseback, negotiating unforgiving tracks and harsh environments to connect with the Midwestern railroads. When they journeyed together, there was little room for racial prejudice, but Black cowboys were expected to do extra tasks like cooking. They also had to navigate the varied segregation laws in different states.

At the end of a long drive, cowboys would sometimes hold informal competitions to test their skills. These evolved into the modern rodeo, with competitions such as bull riding, team roping, bronc riding, and steer wrestling. For many years, African Americans weren't allowed to own horses and had to get written permission to ride. In the late 1800s, rodeos conformed with local Jim Crow laws, leading to lower pay, racist judging, and other second-class treatment of Black riders. However, many pioneering stars were African American, such as Bill Pickett, who invented bulldogging, a form of steer wrestling.

In the late 20th and early 21st centuries, Black characters finally started appearing in Hollywood Westerns like *Posse* and *Django Unchained*. Across the US, there are several organizations keeping Black cowboy history alive, like the Arizona Black Rodeo and the National Multicultural Western Heritage Museum. Trail drives are still popular, too, celebrating a mixture of horse-riding, rodeo, and dancing.

Nat Love, a talented roper, also known as 'Deadwood Dick', in South Dakota, 1876

A cowgirl participating in the barrel race competition at the Bill Pickett Invitational Rodeo on April 1, 2017 in Memphis, Tennessee. The Bill Pickett Rodeo celebrates Western heritage and the contributions that Black cowboys and cowgirls have made to rodeo

© Getty

A woodcut showing Black children in a schoolhouse in Charleston, South Carolina, after emancipation

In 1870, the Fifteenth Amendment guaranteed everyone the right to vote regardless of "race, color, or previous condition of servitude"

THE FIFTEENTH AMENDMENT.
CELEBRATED MAY 19th 1870.

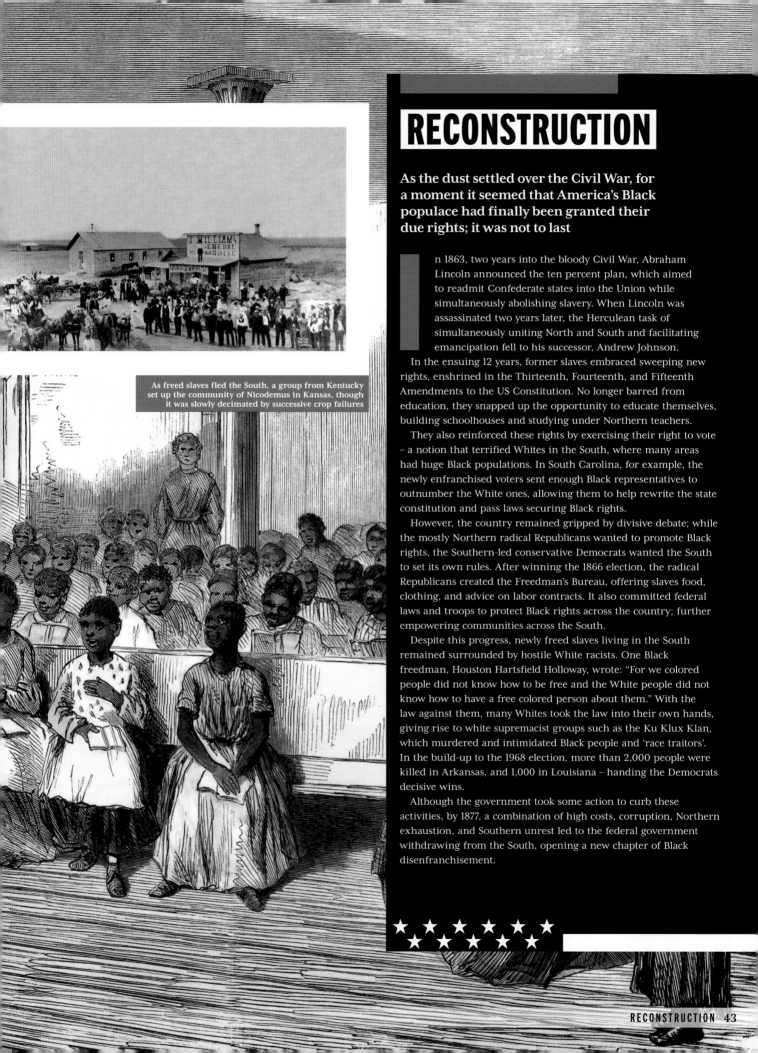

As freed slaves fled the South, a group from Kentucky set up the community of Nicodemus in Kansas, though it was slowly decimated by successive crop failures

RECONSTRUCTION

As the dust settled over the Civil War, for a moment it seemed that America's Black populace had finally been granted their due rights; it was not to last

n 1863, two years into the bloody Civil War, Abraham Lincoln announced the ten percent plan, which aimed to readmit Confederate states into the Union while simultaneously abolishing slavery. When Lincoln was assassinated two years later, the Herculean task of simultaneously uniting North and South and facilitating emancipation fell to his successor, Andrew Johnson.

In the ensuing 12 years, former slaves embraced sweeping new rights, enshrined in the Thirteenth, Fourteenth, and Fifteenth Amendments to the US Constitution. No longer barred from education, they snapped up the opportunity to educate themselves, building schoolhouses and studying under Northern teachers.

They also reinforced these rights by exercising their right to vote – a notion that terrified Whites in the South, where many areas had huge Black populations. In South Carolina, for example, the newly enfranchised voters sent enough Black representatives to outnumber the White ones, allowing them to help rewrite the state constitution and pass laws securing Black rights.

However, the country remained gripped by divisive debate; while the mostly Northern radical Republicans wanted to promote Black rights, the Southern-led conservative Democrats wanted the South to set its own rules. After winning the 1866 election, the radical Republicans created the Freedman's Bureau, offering slaves food, clothing, and advice on labor contracts. It also committed federal laws and troops to protect Black rights across the country; further empowering communities across the South.

Despite this progress, newly freed slaves living in the South remained surrounded by hostile White racists. One Black freedman, Houston Hartsfield Holloway, wrote: "For we colored people did not know how to be free and the White people did not know how to have a free colored person about them." With the law against them, many Whites took the law into their own hands, giving rise to white supremacist groups such as the Ku Klux Klan, which murdered and intimidated Black people and 'race traitors'. In the build-up to the 1968 election, more than 2,000 people were killed in Arkansas, and 1,000 in Louisiana – handing the Democrats decisive wins.

Although the government took some action to curb these activities, by 1877, a combination of high costs, corruption, Northern exhaustion, and Southern unrest led to the federal government withdrawing from the South, opening a new chapter of Black disenfranchisement.

THE JIM CROW LAWS

After the Civil War, slavery was simply replaced by another racist system, designed to subjugate and oppress Black people through a mosaic of local laws, codes, and agreements

ollowing the Civil War, the US Constitution was revised to abolish slavery, while providing citizenship and guaranteeing the right to vote for Black people. However, the Supreme Court worked tirelessly to undermine this progress, ruling in 1883 that while states could not discriminate against African Americans, private citizens could. This paved the way for the legitimization of racism via a tapestry of racist state and local laws, codes, and agreements, designed to restrict the rights of Black people, known as the 'Jim Crow' laws – named after a famous 19th-century White minstrel, who performed racist shows in blackface.

While laws and circumstances varied across different parts of the country, in many of the US's towns and communities, they formed a bulwark of segregation, dividing Black and White people in all aspects of society. They destined Black people were for lives of inequality; born in their own hospitals, buried in their own graveyards, educated in their own schools, and entertained in their own leisure facilities. 'Whites only' signs were commonplace, strewn over bus stations, water fountains, toilets, and buildings, denying Black people the right to access decent services, based on their skin color alone.

Anyone believed to have a Black ancestor could be turned away from White-only parks, theaters, or restaurants, reinforcing a status quo where Whites were seen as superior to Black people. It was even illegal for Black people and White people to marry.

Despite technically having the right to vote, Black people were restricted from doing anything to reverse the Jim Crow laws by the poll tax, fraud, literacy tests and, when all else failed, violence. Adding a further barrier, the 'grandfather clause' stipulated that only people whose grandfathers had voted were eligible to vote – making engagement in democracy impossible for the descendants of slaves.

The Jim Crow laws lasted well beyond World War II, and only began to become undone with President Harry Truman's 1948 executive order eliminating racial discrimination from the military. However, it would be another two decades before they were formally reversed by the Civil Rights and Voting Rights Acts of 1964 and 1965.

A Black man drinking at a 'Colored' water cooler in Oklahoma, 1939

Prison is Better Than Army Jimcrow Service

GATE 2 GATE 2

WE DEM
AN EX
ORDE
MILI

For America's Black veterans, racial segregation in the armed forces was a particularly bitter pill to swallow

© Alamy, Getty

WASHINGTON AND DU BOIS: THE POWER OF EDUCATION

Although their views were radically different, Booker T. Washington and W.E.B. Du Bois both played crucial roles in empowering Black Americans through education

Born the son of a Black slave, Booker T. Washington inherited his mother's chains; without even a family name. After the Civil War, having secured his freedom at the age of nine, he moved to West Virginia, where he adopted step-father's surname 'Washington' upon ering grammar school. He later worked at alt furnace, before studying at the Hampton rmal and Agriculture Institute, and then yland Seminary. Hampton left such an pression that he became convinced the only ble path for Black people to achieve success s through vocational training.

n 1881, he moved to Alabama to become Tuskegee Normal and Industrial Institute's t principal. Expanding the Hampton model, shington hoped to establish a system to ip Black people with the vocational skills uired to entrench themselves into the idly developing economy through high-ality labor.

hrough his work at Tuskegee, Washington n over several prominent White employers governors, who liked that his style of cation would provide a steady stream of or, while simultaneously keeping Black people confined 'down on the farm' and in particular trades. By infusing this ethos with a Protestant work ethic, he broadened his appeal with Northern millionaires such as Rockefeller and Carnegie, procuring enough support to transform Tuskegee into the country's best-supported Black educational facility.

He sincerely believed its model would pave the way for Black people to escape sharecropping and debt, to achieve somewhat of a meaningful life as self-employed individuals, small businesspeople, and perhaps even land owners. In exchange, they would simply have to learn to adapt to an unjust, authoritarian hierarchy, within which they occupied the lowest rungs. With this in mind, he felt that Black education should "be so directed that the greatest proportion of the mental strength of the masses will be brought to bear upon the everyday practical things of life, upon something that is needed to be done, and something which they will be permitted to do in the community in which they reside."

Washington was catapulted to fame by his September 1895 speech, 'The Atlanta Compromise', where he appealed to White America: "I pledge that in your effort to work out the great and intricate problem which God has laid at the doors of the South, you shall have at all times the patient, sympathetic help of my race; only let this be constantly in mind, that, while from representations in these buildings of the product of field, of forest, of mine, of factory, letters, and art, much good will come, yet far above and beyond material benefits will be that higher good, that, let us pray God, will come, in a blotting out of sectional differences and racial animosities and suspicions, in a determination to administer absolute justice, in a willing obedience among all classes to the mandates of law. This, coupled with our material prosperity, will bring into our beloved South a new heaven and a new earth."

Building on his efforts to secure a 'Compromise', he wrote a well-received autobiography, *Up From Slavery* in 1901, founded

Emerging from the Reconstruction, Black educator Booker T. Washington, pictured with President Theodore Roosevelt, called for 'Compromise'; a notion that would soon give way to direct action

the National Negro Business League, and served as chief Black advisor to Presidents Theodore Roosevelt and William Howard Taft. His views represented those of many of the Reconstruction-era's educated Black population. White Americans, they believed, admired financial success in the capitalist system above all else; if Black people could demonstrate their ability to acquire wealth and respectability within the constraints of the system, they would earn the respect of their White peers and slowly rise to their equals.

Unfortunately this didn't happen. By the turn of the 20th century, even in the North, Black business owners found White customers growing increasingly reluctant to support them – driving many into bankruptcy. However, as increasing numbers of Black people fled

Washington believed that Black people should focus on becoming financially viable through industrial vocational training, and wait for discrimination to slowly subside

the brutal racism of the South, increasing urbanization facilitated the spread of Black-owned businesses, catering to Black customers. It was this environment that gave rise to the real estate magnate, Robert Reed Church and the legendary Madam C.J. Walker, inventor of the straightening comb, and the first Black female millionaire.

Amidst the changing climate, Washington's ideas began to encounter resistance from a growing group of Black academics and professionals with a radically different perspective: the Niagara Movement. Founded by the intellectual giant, William Edward Burghardt Du Bois, the Movement called for "full citizenship rights for Blacks and public recognition of their contributions to America's stability and progress." This was in stark contrast to Washington's stance, who they dubbed 'The Great Accommodator'. The Movement were no longer willing to simply accept the status quo of lynchings, segregation, and racist segregation laws.

Despite Washington's efforts to mitigate racism by secretly financing civil suits and procuring aid for Black colleges, his approach had failed to improve the wider issues of racial discrimination. At the time of his death, the tide was beginning to turn in favor of Du Bois' ideas. Born a free man in 1868 Massachusetts to a White French father and a Black mother, Du Bois grew into an unprecedented intellectual

The first Black man to obtain a PhD in social sciences from Harvard, Du Bois emphasized the importance of liberal arts

Washington's philosophy of compromise earned huge levels of financial support from White philanthropists, transforming Tuskegee into the country's best established Black educational facility

force of the times; attending Fisk University, before becoming the first Black person to receive a PhD in social sciences at Harvard. Responding to Washington's Compromise, he wrote *The Souls of Black Folk* – envisioning a

future time where culture was dominated by Black consciousness, solidarity, and activists creating a paradigm shift.

Emphasizing the importance of a classic liberal arts education, Du Bois believed that

Unwilling to passively accept discrimination, the NAACP engaged in direct action, such as 1917's 10,000-person Silent Parade, protesting against racist lynchings and violence

Washington celebrates the 25th anniversary of the Tuskegee Institute with Robert C. Ogden (left), secretary of war William Taft, and Andrew Carnegie (right)

MARCUS GARVEY

A radical Jamaican firebrand who dreamed of uniting all Black people of the world, Marcus Garvey's ideas were considered too radical to simply go unchecked

Born in 1887 in Jamaica's St. Ann's Bay, after leaving school at 14, Marcus Garvey spent time with Jamaican nationalist groups, before touring Central America and London. Inspired by Booker T. Washington, he hoped to open his own industrial training school, and traveled to the US to meet his idol; who unfortunately died just before his arrival. However, as he lectured across the US, gripped by race riots, he steered course, creating a chapter of his Jamaican group, the Universal Negro Improvement Association (UNIA), in New York.

A powerful orator and organizer, he merged Jamaican peasant aspirations for independence with America's gospel of success, centered around the right for all Black people to return to Africa. The result was a philosophy of pan-African solidarity and self-empowerment. These ideas were vital in the formation of Rastafarianism.

By 1920, Garvey's UNIA group had hundreds of chapters worldwide, a shipping line linking the US, Caribbean, and Africa, and a weekly publication, notoriously banned in various countries. His relentless approach earned the ire of the Bureau of Investigation, who hired the FBI's first Black agent to infiltrate and sabotage the Black Star shipping line. After being indicted on mail fraud charges and deported back to Jamaica in 1927, Garvey descended into obscurity, dying in 1940.

the Black community could only achieve social justice and equality through the efforts of an intellectual vanguard of college-educated Black, who he called the 'Talented Tenth': "The Negro Race, like all races, is going to be saved by its exceptional men. The problem of education then, among Negroes, must first of all deal with the 'Talented Tenth'. It is the problem of developing the best of this race that they may guide the Mass away from the contamination and death of the worst."

Reflecting his more direct demeanor, he added, "Men of America, the problem is plain before you. Here is a race transplanted through the criminal foolishness of your fathers. Whether you like it or not the millions are here, and here they will remain." As finances and membership for the Niagara Movement dwindled, the group survived by morphing into a direct action-orientated group called the National Association for the Advancement of Colored People (NAACP), which was established in 1909. This change sowed the seeds of the Civil Rights Movement to come.

As the editor of the NAACP's monthly

magazine *The Crisis*, and as one of the organization's most prominent leaders, Du Bois continued to actively promote and protest discrimination on behalf of all Black Americans. However, as his ideas snowballed into the Civil Rights Movement, he became increasingly disillusioned with the nation, and its Black elites. This came to a head in 1951, when he was arrested and arraigned as a Soviet agent as part of the McCarthyism movement, for circulating a petition protesting nuclear weapons. Despite being acquitted, Du Bois was left penniless and had his passport revoked – when it was finally returned, he moved to the newly independent nation of Ghana. After his departure, the US – the nation where he was born, and for which he had sacrificed so much – revoked his passport once again. He died a Ghanaian citizen in 1963, on the eve of the March on Washington.

Though he and Washington had clashed over the best way to proceed, each played a crucial role in laying down the intellectual foundation for the Civil Rights Movement, and paving the path to a new world of opportunity.

> ## "DU BOIS CONTINUED TO ACTIVELY PROMOTE AND PROTEST DISCRIMINATION ON BEHALF OF ALL BLACK AMERICANS"

A fiery orator, Marcus Garvey's ideas gave rise to the Pan-African movement, laying the groundwork for the Jamaican religion, Rastafarianism

The 20th annual meeting of the NAACP in Cleveland, Ohio, in 1929

NAACP leaders Henry L. Moon, Roy Wilkins, Herbert Hill, and Thurgood Marshall campaigning against racial violence in Mississippi in 1956

STAMP OUT MISSISSIPPI-ISM!

JOIN NAACP

NATIONAL ASSOCIATION FOR THE ADVANCEMENT OF COLORED PEOPLE

THE NAACP IS FOUNDED

Established as a necessary tool in the fight for civil rights in 1909, the NAACP is still going strong after more than a century

A defiant plan to tackle racial injustice arose from the Springfield race riots of 1908. The unification of a group of White liberals and notable African Americans, such as Ida B. Wells and W.E.B. Du Bois, led to the formation of the National Association for the Advancement of Colored People (NAACP), America's largest and most recognized civil rights organization, in February 1909.

As part of its mission to advance the interests of Black citizens, the NAACP aimed to eradicate racial discrimination and guarantee the rights of African Americans to education, employment, and the vote. As director of publications and research, in 1910, Du Bois co-founded *The Crisis*, the NAACP's acclaimed publication.

Within four years, the NAACP had branched out of New York to cities across the US. The model of local grassroots recruitment of members, fundraising, and campaigning was hugely effective. The NAACP's legal advocacy in rallying against separate-but-equal doctrines helped end segregated education, while its anti-lynching campaign was also crucial in raising public awareness of the issue and contributed to a decline in lynchings across the South.

But the NAACP paid dearly for its successes. On Christmas Day of 1951, NAACP field secretary Harry T. Moore and his wife were murdered when their home was bombed. Another field secretary, Medgar Evers, was assassinated in 1963 after years of persecution against him and his wife, Myrlie Evers (who became the third woman to chair the NAACP in 1995). The NAACP also faced hostility from those who felt they should favor more direct action. During the civil rights era, the NAACP supported Freedom Riders and helped to organize the 1963 March on Washington. Such collaboration led to the 1964 Civil Rights Act.

During this period, notable celebrities embraced and supported the NAACP, including Sammy Davis Jr., Lena Horne, Jackie Robinson, and Harry Belafonte. Today, Beyoncé and her Beygood Foundation partner with the NAACP to provide grants for Black-owned businesses, while the NAACP Image Awards maintain the ties to Hollywood.

With 2,200 volunteer-run branches and more than two million members across the US, the NAACP continues to fight against student debt, police brutality, the climate crisis, and voter apathy as part of its campaign for social and economic justice.

The NAACP's Roy Wilkins and Medgar Evers are arrested in Jackson, Mississippi in 1963. Evers would be assassinated later that year

in African-American politics. Poets such as Countee Cullen addressed their African heritage in their works, and artists like the Kansas-born painter Aaron Douglas used African motifs in their art. A number of musicians, including the jazz legend Louis Armstrong, introduced African-inspired rhythms and themes into their compositions. Zora Neale Hurston explored rural Southern Black life – using her knowledge and experience as a folklorist – in her 1937 novel, *Their Eyes Were Watching God*.

The photographer James Van Der Zee documented African-American life in Harlem through his images – some formal, some candid shots taken in Harlem's cabarets, restaurants and neighborhoods. He became the unofficial chronicler of a diverse and thriving community. Many poets, including Langston Hughes and Claude McKay, drew on Harlem life for their verses, and McKay also used it as the setting for his first novel, *Home to Harlem*.

The impact of race and racism on African Americans was a key theme of the Harlem Renaissance. McKay's poem, "If We Must Die" (1919) – "If we must die, let it not be like hogs / Hunted and penned in an inglorious spot. . ." –

was written in response to mob attacks against African Americans during the 'Red Summer' of 1919 when there were dozens of racist attacks across the country over a few months. Much of the literature of the Harlem Renaissance avoided overt protest, and instead focused on the psychological and social impacts of race and racism, such as Nella Larsen's novels – *Quicksand* (1928) and *Passing* (1929) – which both included characters of mixed heritage who struggled to define their identity in a racist world. Langston Hughes addressed similar themes in his 1931 play, *Mulatto*.

The Harlem Renaissance has sometimes been referred to as the 'New Negro Movement', epitomized in *The New Negro*, an anthology edited by Alain Locke (1925). The publication featured many of the big names in literature and poetry at the time, such as Countee Cullen, Rudolph Fisher, and Jean Toomer, and presented a new African American who was proud, assertive, and self-confident, unafraid to experiment and express themselves. W.E.B. Du Bois (1868-1963) took the opportunity to present Black Americans to White America with his story 'The Black Man Brings His Gifts' and

Langston Hughes encourages the Black youth to rise together in their self-expression and claim their bright future, in his poem "Youth."

In 1926, a group of Black artists – including Wallace

Thurman, Zora Neale Hurston, John P Davis, Gwendolyn Bennett, and Langston Hughes – created a literary magazine called *Fire!!*, subtitled 'A Quarterly devoted to the Younger Negro Artists'. The group, who

An illustration by Winold Reiss from page 269 of *The New Negro* edited by Alain Locke

also sometimes referred to themselves, with irony, as 'The Niggerati', intended to 'scandalize the elders' and express the changing attitudes of young African Americans. *Fire!!* explored controversial issues in the Black community, such as sexuality, interracial relationships, prostitution, and colorism. The journal was heavily critiqued, but some celebrated its unique personality and diverse content. After just one issue, though, its quarters burned down and the magazine ended.

As the creative scene blossomed in Harlem, and elsewhere, more and more White folks began to take notice. Suddenly White Americans were major consumers of Black art, and Black artists had an opportunity they hadn't had before – to be heard and seen by mainstream America. This created a dilemma for Black

The writer Zora Neale Hurston (1891-1960) at a book fair, New York, circa 1937

"BLACK ARTISTS HAD AN OPPORTUNITY THEY HADN'T HAD BEFORE – TO BE HEARD AND SEEN BY MAINSTREAM AMERICA"

Performers on stage during a dance routine at the Cotton Club in Harlem in 1934 artists and there were many debates in the community about who Black art was produced for – purely for the entertainment of White audiences? Or should the focus be the experience of fellow Black people?

The Cotton Club was a legendary nightclub in Harlem that showcased Black entertainers and performers to White audiences, and was the springboard to fame for musicians such as Duke Ellington, Louis Armstrong, Fats Waller, Adelaide Hall, Bessie Smith, The Mills Brothers, and Billie Holiday. The Cotton Club was a 'Whites-only' establishment, and Black people were only allowed in as performers or workers, with rare exceptions made for celebrities. Many other aspects of the club supported the racism of the era, with menus depicting imagery of naked Black men and women as savages in an exotic jungle and tribal mask illustrations around the border.

The Harlem Renaissance brought the Black experience clearly into the White consciousness, and demonstrated the founding role that African Americans had played in the formation of the American cultural landscape. On a sociological level, it redefined how America, and the world, viewed African Americans. The full political consequences were arguably not apparent until the emergence of the Civil Rights Movement in the 1950s, when there was a renewed interest in the works of the Harlem Renaissance.

As a literary movement alone, the Harlem Renaissance laid the groundwork for all African-American literature that followed, and had a crucial impact on Black literature worldwide. The work of writers such as Claude McKay, Jean Toomer, and Wallace Thurman were both inspired by and fed the commercial growth of jazz music and a simultaneous flourishing of work by Black visual artists such as Aaron Douglas, Laura Wheeler Waring, and Jacob Lawrence.

It is hard to pinpoint a precise beginning or end of the Harlem Renaissance. In some ways, it gradually faded away in the late 1930s and early 1940s during the Great Depression, when a lot of the venues closed down and people simply didn't have the disposable income to purchase art, theater tickets, or magazine subscriptions. The 1935 Harlem Race Riot – which erupted after the death of a young Puerto Rican boy in police custody – also lifted the veil on bubbling frustrations. In spite of the presence of artists, nightclubs and entertainment, Harlem had become a place characterized by racial discrimination and poverty. Although musicians, poets, and artists would continue to make their home there, Harlem gradually became less of a focal point of a creative movement. However, the ripples of expression and understanding that the Harlem Renaissance period created are still expanding today, and contribute a vital chapter in both African-American culture and Black culture worldwide.

Jazz singer Billie Holiday and composer Duke Ellington rehearse 'Symphony in Black: A Rhapsody of Negro Life' in 1935

© Getty, Wikimedia Commons

"AS GAY AS IT WAS BLACK"

The freedom of expression and experimentation that was encouraged on the Harlem scene of the 1920s wasn't all centered around creativity, it also included sexuality

Although not always acknowledged in the history books, many of the Harlem Renaissance key players were openly gay or identified as having nuanced sexualities – including Angelina Weld Grimké, Claude McKay, and Alice Dunbar-Nelson among others. Many more have been widely speculated about, such as Langston Hughes. In Harlem in the 1920s and 1930s there was "a sense of new possibilities," as Octavio R. González, a professor at Wellesley College and an expert on the Harlem Renaissance, explains, "Sexuality became a form of freedom. . . expressing sexuality became a form of emancipation."

During the 1920s in Harlem, and indeed around the country, more and more people rebelled against the restrictions of Prohibition. The speakeasy culture of the time laid the foundations for LGBTQ+ nightlife and drag balls, which Langston Hughes described as "Spectacles in Color."

Blues singer and pianist, Gladys Bentley (1907–60), was known for singing raunchy songs in a deep, growling voice and dressing in men's suits. For many years, she regularly filled venues with loud, rowdy performances, during which she

Gladys Bentley (pictured here, circa 1930) is now widely celebrated for the Black female masculinity that she exuded

flirted with women in the audience. She claimed, during an interview with a gossip columnist, that she had married a White woman. Although there's no record of the union taking place, this kind of unapologetic openness about sexuality – especially one with all the makings of an early 20th-century scandal – was unheard of at the time.

One of the openly gay Black writers of the time, Richard Bruce Nugent, published a short story, "Smoke, Lilies and Jade", which became considered a seminal work of gay Harlem. In it, Nugent explores bisexuality and depicts homosexual relationships between artists.

Historian, Henry Louis Gates Jr., described the Harlem Renaissance as being "surely as gay as it was black."

THE TULSA RACE MASSACRE

In 1921, bitter White resentment consumed America's most prosperous Black community, culminating in a bloody massacre that left 'Black Wall Street' in ashes

A t the end of World War I, the city of Tulsa, Oklahoma, hosted one of the United States' most prosperous Black communities, centered around the Greenwood District, nicknamed 'Black Wall Street'. The area was a rare beacon of hope and opportunity for the country's oppressed Black populace, who had built their own commercial and residential center, home to around 10,000 people. With its own cinemas, banks, hotels, nightclubs, billiard halls, groceries, and amenities, it was a remarkably self-sufficient community; a source of bitter resentment for the region's White racists.

Those tensions boiled over on May 31, 1921, when the *Tulsa Tribune* ran a notorious story, alleging that a Black man named Dick Rowland had attempted to sexually assault a White woman. It didn't take long for a White mob to gather outside the courthouse, where the sheriff had barricaded Rowland inside. Concerned that Rowland was in danger of being lynched, some Black supporters showed up; but before long, people began firing guns, and the Black group fled into Greenwood.

Enraged and thirsty for blood, the White mob chased them down, and began murdering Black people on sight, looting their buildings and setting them ablaze. As Black Wall Street burned, the governor declared martial law, but when the National Guard arrived, instead of arresting the rioters they rounded up the city's 6,000 Black residents and confined them to the Convention Hall and Fairgrounds; some of the troops even joining in the violence.

After 24 hours of bloodlust and chaos, Greenwood lay in ruins; 35 city blocks had been burned to the ground, 800 people injured and hundreds more killed; 10,000 left homeless. Some Black residents were kept in confinement for eight days and after all of the brutality, the charges against Rowland were dropped. Although some sympathetic White people from the region offered assistance, alongside the American Red Cross, none of the rioters were ever prosecuted. Instead, Tulsa authorities covered up the incident, placing its victims in unmarked graves and destroying police records, alongside the inflammatory *Tribune* article that had kicked it all off.

Before the race riots, Greenwood was home to several successful Black entrepreneurs, such as John Wesley Williams, pictured with his wife, Loula, and son WD

After the massacre, rather than attempting to pursue justice, the local Tulsa authorities simply covered the event up, destroying police records and burying victims in unmarked graves

Almost 200 businesses were
destroyed and more than
1,000 homes set on fire

JESSE OWENS

An African-American athlete humiliated the Nazi regime yet still faced discrimination in his homeland

Jesse Owens' unlikely friendship with German long jumper Luz Long was snuffed out when Long was killed in action in 1943

Adolf Hitler hoped the 1936 Olympics in Berlin would be a propaganda masterpiece offering tangible proof of Aryan supremacy on the sports field. He envisaged German athletes standing proud as the national anthem echoed around the Olympiastadion, but the athlete who came to embody the Games was anything but the Nazi ideal.

Jesse Owens, the youngest of ten children born to an Alabama sharecropper, displayed his athletic prowess early in life. He equalled the world record for the 100-yard dash while still in high school. Two years later, while competing for Ohio State University, he set three world records and equalled another in less than an hour.

A year later, Owens was a hot favorite to win gold at his first (and only) Olympics. He did not disappoint. Owens placed first in the 100 meters. The next day, he won the long jump despite fouling on his first two attempts. Owens later claimed that advice from a German, Luz Long, helped him to land his third jump and earn a place in the final. Long ended up with the silver medal. Owens gained a third Olympic title in three days when he won the 200 meters and picked up a fourth later in the Games as part of the 4x100m relay.

Owens was a surprisingly popular winner. The German crowd cheered each victory and young fans were desperate to meet him. A legend subsequently emerged that Hitler refused to congratulate Owens. However, the German leader shook the hands of the German victors only on the first day. When the IOC president insisted that he congratulate victors from either all nations or none from day two (when Owens won his first gold medal), Hitler opted for the latter.

One world leader who did snub the four-time champion was US president Franklin D. Roosevelt. Owens was not invited to the White House to celebrate his achievement and, following a tickertape parade in New York, was not permitted to use the main entrance to the Waldorf Astoria and sent to a service lift. Owens pointedly contrasted the way he was feted in Nazi Germany and the segregation he faced in his supposedly free homeland.

Owens received a hero's welcome upon his return to the USA yet still faced racial discrimination

© Getty

THE BLACK EXPERIENCE IN WORLD WAR II

Although they endured segregation and discrimination at home and abroad, Black Americans contributed to victory in World War II

expansion. Black Americans served during the Spanish-American War and experienced the privations of the Western Front during World War I, 1917-18.

A generation later, as the United States prepared for war against Imperial Japan, Nazi Germany and Fascist Italy, such contributions had largely been relegated to footnotes in the pages of American history. Prejudice, segregation, lack of opportunity, and the specter of poverty still haunted the Black experience in America – citizens, yes; full citizens, a resounding no. In the South, the long arm of Jim Crow restricted freedoms; across the nation public facilities were separate, and signs blaring 'White only' were commonplace.

Therefore, as the US girded for war a continuing question emerged: How exactly would the Black population participate in the coming fight – if at all? The great irony persisted. Those who had been denied the full flower of equality at home might well be asked to give their lives in combat against oppressive regimes in foreign countries for the freedom of others.

The voices of Black Americans raised conflicting viewpoints. Patriotism, right versus wrong, and the inherent inequality of the 'system' weighed heavily on the discourse.

After the United States was plunged into World War II following the Japanese attack on Pearl Harbor on December 7, 1941, labor advocate

are citizens of the United States and must proudly and bravely assume the responsibilities and duties of American citizens. . . Without democracy in America, limited though it may be, the Negro would not have even the right to fight for his rights."

Other Black leaders disagreed. "Democracy will not and cannot be safe in America as long as ten percent of its population is deprived of its rights, privileges, and immunities plainly granted to them by the Constitution of the United States," observed Arthur Spingarn, president of the National Association for the Advancement of Colored People (NAACP).

THE STRUGGLE TO SERVE

Even before US entry into the war, the question of Black participation was prominent. The armed forces remained segregated, and only the Army and Navy were allowed to accept Black enlistees, but the roles of those accepted were limited to service endeavors such as cooks and transport responsibilities. Prior to World War II, thousands of Black men had tried to enter the service only to be denied.

> "PRIOR TO WORLD WAR II, THOUSANDS OF BLACK MEN HAD TRIED TO ENTER THE SERVICE ONLY TO BE DENIED"

mobilized in the summer of 1941, jobs were created, but Black Americans were often barred from them. In response, Randolph organized a march on Washington to protest the systemic discrimination in both military and civilian life. On June 25, 1941, President Franklin D. Roosevelt issued Executive Order 8802, which banned such unequal treatment in defense industries. Nevertheless, the government effort to end discrimination remained hollow.

As for the armed forces, full desegregation did not become the order of the day until July 26, 1948, three years after World War II ended. President Harry Truman signed Executive Order 9980, which required fair employment practices in federal government agencies. In tandem, Executive Order 9981 decreed, "equality of treatment and opportunity for all personnel without regard to race, color, religion, or national origin." Although Truman's actions did not immediately resolve the issues of racial inequality in America, they did serve as recognition of changing times.

Battery A of the segregated 452nd Antiaircraft Artillery Battalion is shown in France in November 1944

Phyllis Mae Dailey (fifth from left), the first Black servicewoman of World War II, is sworn into the US Navy Nurse Corps

Fleet Admiral Chester W Nimitz presents the Navy Cross to Cook Third Class Doris Miller

Tuskegee Airmen, like this group in Italy, built up legendary status with their military prowess

THE BUSINESS AT HAND

Meanwhile, there was a war on. From 1941 to 1945, a total of 2.5 million Black men registered for the draft, and over a million were accepted into the armed forces. Thousands of Black women responded as well. More than 4,000 students and faculty members at Howard University, a historically Black college in Washington, D.C., volunteered for the service. During the conflict, African Americans served in all military theaters around the world. Despite their contribution, the military establishment was skeptical of a Black soldier's ability to perform in combat or to discharge the duties of officer rank. Those Black Americans who obtained officer rank could not command White soldiers – only other Blacks.

The burgeoning Black experience in World War II gave impetus to the open discussion of race relations, particularly as the Black service personnel deployed to Great Britain and continental Europe typically experienced better treatment overseas than at home. In 1942, James G. Thompson, a young Black soldier, wrote to the Pittsburgh Courier, a Black newspaper, with the burning question: "Should I sacrifice my life to live half American?" Thompson suggested that two victories should be achieved. "The first V for a victory over our enemies from without, the second V for a victory over our enemies from within." The letter was the beginning of the Double V Campaign, which raised the profile of the Black soldier and his contribution to the war effort, while exposing the widespread discrimination that persisted in the armed forces, as well as in everyday life at home.

Despite the headwinds of discrimination, Black soldiers achieved notable successes during World War II, both as service troops and in combat.

Their saga in wartime began at Pearl Harbor as Navy Cook Third Class Doris Miller, aboard the stricken battleship USS West Virginia, moved his mortally wounded captain to safety and then manned a .50-caliber machine gun, firing back boldly at the Japanese attackers. Miller received the Navy Cross for heroism. It was the Navy's second-highest decoration for valor, and he may well have been denied the Medal of Honor simply because of his race.

Elsewhere, the 332nd Fighter Group, nicknamed the 'Tuskegee Airmen' for the Alabama location where they had learned to fly, became legendary in the skies over Europe. Flying the Curtiss P-40 Warhawk and North American P-51 Mustang fighters, the Tuskegee Airmen flew 1,600 combat sorties, escorting bombers during missions over German-occupied territory and shooting down 37 enemy planes while destroying 237 on the ground. The 761st Tank Battalion, nicknamed the 'Black Panthers', fought on the Western Front with the Third Army under the command of General George S. Patton Jr. During more than six months on the front line, these tank soldiers participated in the liberation of 30 towns and cities in Western Europe. Staff Sergeant Ruben Rivers of the Black Panthers received the Medal of Honor for heroism in combat November 15-19, 1944. The posthumous presentation was held in 1997, more than 50 years after the fact.

For 83 crucial days during the Allied dash towards the German frontier in 1944, teams of Black truck drivers kept fuel supplies rolling towards the front lines, driving long hours, much of the time at night, and earning the nickname of the 'Red Ball Express'. Twentieth century Buffalo Soldiers of the 92nd Infantry Division fought the Nazis in Italy, while the 93rd Division deployed to combat zones in the Pacific. And there were many, many others.

> "THE MILITARY ESTABLISHMENT WAS SKEPTICAL OF A BLACK SOLDIER'S ABILITY TO PERFORM IN COMBAT"

African American Marines, service personnel who picked up rifles and went into combat, take a break on Peleliu

MARINES IN COMBAT AT PELELIU

During the bitter fight for a Pacific island, Black Marines from a service unit picked up rifles and fought the Japanese

General William Rupertus, commander of the 1st Marine Division, declared, "Rough but fast. . . We'll be through in three days. It might only take two." The assault on the Pacific island of Peleliu was supposed to conclude swiftly. Instead, the fight with the Japanese defenders in the summer of 1944 became a meat grinder. To say Rupertus had been mistaken is a profound understatement, but early in the fight, his combat Marines got help from an unexpected source.

African-American Marines of the 11th Depot and 7th Ammunition Companies were busy as the combat units hit the beaches. They were unloading crates of ammunition and recovering the bodies of dead Marines along the shoreline. However, as casualties mounted and the need for more riflemen arose, these service Marines picked up weapons and went into the line. A Marine was a Marine, well trained to fight. Shoulder to shoulder with White Marines, they fought the Japanese, displaying great heroism.

In the aftermath of Peleliu, Rupertus commended the Black Marines, writing, "The Negro race can well be proud of the work performed. . . The wholehearted co-operation and untiring efforts which demonstrated in every respect that they appreciated the privilege of wearing a Marine uniform and serving with the Marines in combat. Please convey to your command these sentiments and inform them that in the eyes of the entire Division they have earned a 'well done'."

INTO THE FUTURE

Although their exploits may have evolved in the shadows of the larger conflict, the contributions of Black military personnel to the ultimate victory in World War II are undeniable. Black soldiers who returned from overseas or were discharged after service in the States remained subject to discrimination, many of them denied the benefits of the postwar GI Bill and compelled to endure race-related hostility, which sometimes erupted in violence. Nevertheless, their perspective on the world had changed, and a robust identity as Americans deserving of the fullness of citizenship was fostered.

Some historians point to the Black experience in World War II as the beginning of the Civil Rights Movement that surged across the US during the 1950s and 1960s. Whether the beginning or a continuation of the long struggle, that experience was certainly a window for veterans on a wider world, a catalyst for the redress of systemic racism and discrimination in a democratic country, where personal freedom and full citizenship remain watchwords of equality and opportunity.

Two Black soldiers taking a moment to pose with their personalized messages to Hitler

LEVELING THE PLAYING FIELD

Black athletes have been breaking down barriers in US sport ever since Jackie Robinson took to the baseball diamond

Batting second for the Brooklyn Dodgers, the debutant swung his bat but did not get a good connection on the pitched ball. The leather sphere bounced once before it was gathered by the fielder at third base. He threw hard to his colleague at first base to record the out before the batsman got anywhere close.

As sporting debuts go, it was unspectacular. But for the wider history of American sport, it was remarkable. The 26,623 spectators gathered at Ebbets Field on April 10, 1947 had just witnessed Major League Baseball's first Black player in the 20th century. Jackie Robinson had made his way into the history books.

PLAYING BALL

Racial segregation had existed in baseball since the end of the 20th century when clubs and leagues voted to ban contracts with the small number of active African-American players. The only other option the Black players had was to join one of the Negro leagues. They were organized affairs – the champions from various Negro leagues met in the Colored World Series in the 1920s and the Negro World Series in the 1940s – but they were still regarded as inferior to the Major League.

Attempts to reintegrate baseball were doomed to fail as long as Kenesaw Mountain Landis remained commissioner of baseball. However, his death in 1944 removed one of the most determined opponents of African-American baseballers joining the Major League.

His successor, Happy Chandler, was open to integration. Holding a similar mindset was Branch Rickey, general manager of the Brooklyn Dodgers. He had been asking his scouts to find the perfect player to break baseball's color line since the end of World War II.

The man he selected was Jackie Robinson, a shortstop with the Kansas City Monarchs of the Negro American League. Rickey signed him up and sent him to hone his craft with the Montreal Royals, a Dodgers affiliate in the minor leagues. After one season, during which Robinson had the best batting average and was named his league's Most Valuable Player, Rickey was convinced that his controversial signing was ready for the big time.

He certainly was. Robinson batted so well in his debut season in Major League Baseball that he was named Rookie of the Year (although at 28, he was considerably older than most of his fellow first-timers) and helped take the Dodgers to the World Series, which they lost 4-3 to the New York Yankees.

Rickey had considered more than pure baseball talent when he selected Robinson to be the first Black baseballer of modern times. He also wanted to ensure that Robinson had the strength of character to succeed in the full glare of the media spotlight.

Branch Rickey carefully selected Jackie Robinson to be the first Black baseballer; he wanted the right character as well as baseball talent

Eric Reid and Colin Kaepernick's protest against police brutality drew national attention to the influence of Black sportspeople in the USA

Meet the Black athletes who broke down barriers before Jackie Robinson

Marshall Taylor
Cycling

Having worked in bicycle shops as a child, Taylor became a professional rider at the age of 18. Though some organizers refused to let him compete, Taylor won the sprint at the 1899 World Track Championships and became the first Black American world champion in any sport.

Jack Johnson
Boxing

Johnson became boxing's first Black heavyweight champion in 1908 and held the title for seven years. He was hounded by the authorities, partly due to his marriage to three different White women. He was sentenced to a year in prison in 1913 on trumped-up charges by Kenesaw Mountain Landis, the future commissioner of baseball.

Ora Washington
Tennis and basketball

Washington won eight singles titles from the Black-only American Tennis Association and starred for the Philadelphia Tribune basketball team from 1932, leading them to 11 consecutive victories at the Women's Colored World Championships. However, segregation barred her from competing at other tennis events and taking on the world number one, Helen Wills.

Josh Gibson
Baseball

Three months before Jackie Robinson's Major League debut, a player once predicted to be the first Black baseballer died after suffering a stroke at 35. Gibson was a spectacular power hitter who hit around 800 home runs in the Negro leagues and was known as the Black Babe Ruth.

He understood that many Americans were vehemently opposed to integration. Robinson would be denied the ability to stay at the same hotels or eat at the same restaurants as his teammates when traveling in the South. Heckling, racial epithets and death threats were expected. Rickey asked Robinson if he could face racial abuse without anger. Robinson was confused. "Are you looking for a Negro who is afraid to fight back?" he asked. Rickey then replied that he wanted a player "with guts enough not to fight back".

So deep were the roots of racial discrimination that several of his own teammates were uneasy about sharing the field with a Black player, although Rickey and the club management made clear they would back Robinson by trading or releasing White players who caused trouble. Some opposing players reportedly threatened to strike but the commissioner quickly let them know that they would be suspended from baseball if they carried out their threat. When Robinson was racially abused by the player-manager of the Philadelphia Phillies, it galvanized the Dodgers and the team rallied around their player, spurring a run to the World Series.

ISOLATION TO ACCEPTANCE

Within two years, Robinson's right to play ball was widely accepted. In 1949 he was named the National League's Most Valuable Player, chosen by baseball writers, and was voted by fans into the All-Star Team, the first of six consecutive seasons he would be honored. By the time he retired in 1957, Robinson had played in six World Series, winning the 1955 edition and losing the other five to the Yankees.

Robinson was also no longer the sole African-

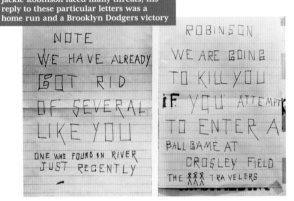

Jackie Robinson faced many threats, his reply to these particular letters was a home run and a Brooklyn Dodgers victory

Willie Mays, who debuted for the New York Giants in 1951, may be the greatest all-round baseballer of all time

American player in baseball. The second, Larry Doby, made his first appearance for the Cleveland Indians in July 1947, three months after Robinson's debut. The following year, Doby and teammate Satchel Paige, another Black player, were part of the Indians team that won the World Series. Nor was Robinson the only Black Brooklyn Dodger. Dan Bankhead joined the team in August 1947 and managed to achieve what Robinson had not – he hit a home run in his first at-bat.

Over the next few years, each of the 16 Major League teams added African-American players to their rosters. The final holdouts were the Boston Red Sox. Despite giving Robinson a trial in April 1945, before he signed for the Dodgers, the Red Sox management was accused of deliberately resisting integration. Some suggested the edict came from owner Tom Yawkey. However, by refusing to employ Black players, the Red Sox missed out on the chance to dip into a talent pool that included Hall of Famers like Hank Aaron and Willie Mays.

By 1981, 18.7 percent of Major League ballplayers were Black Americans. Since then, the proportion has dropped. On the opening day of the 2021 season, seven percent of players on Major League rosters were Black Americans. In the United States as a whole, 13.4 percent of people identify as Black or African American.

The Boston Celtics were the first NBA team to break the quota of Black players; they won the NBA Championship the next three years

SHOOTING HOOPS

Part of the reason why the proportion of Black baseballers has dropped in the past few decades is because of a monumental shift in American sports culture that occurred from the 1960s to the 1990s. African Americans flocked to basketball in huge numbers.

Just over three years after Jackie Robinson played his first game for the Brooklyn Dodgers, Walter Brown, the founder of the Boston Celtics of the National Basketball Association (NBA), announced that he was drafting Charles Cooper from Duquesne University. There was a stunned silence in the room. Finally, one of the other team owners piped up: "Walter, don't you know he's a colored boy?"

Jackie Robinson's success in baseball paved the way for the integration of Black athletes in other sports, but basketball's circle of rich team owners was still wary. Progress was slow. One day before Cooper's debut, Earl Lloyd became the first African American to play in an NBA game when he took to the court for the Washington Capitols on October 31, 1950. However, the number of Black players remained relatively low. No team had more than four Black players on their 12-man rosters before 1963. Of around 100 active players in the 1959-60 season, 18 were Black.

The team owners maintained an unofficial quota system that ensured no team took on too many Black players. When the Philadelphia Warriors wanted to sign promising youngster Al Attles in 1960, it would have meant them carrying five Black players on the roster. Soon after Attles' trial, the Warriors released

Earl Lloyd was the first Black basketballer to play in the NBA when he started for the Washington Capitols on Halloween 1950

> "JACKIE ROBINSON'S SUCCESS IN BASEBALL PAVED THE WAY FOR THE INTEGRATION OF BLACK ATHLETES"

Woody Sauldsberry, the Rookie of the Year in 1958 and an All-Star in 1959. It was a decision that made little sense apart from to uphold an arbitrary quota of Black players. Sauldsberry certainly saw it that way and was reduced to hopping from team to team as a journeyman pro.

However, competition from the rival American Basketball Association in the mid-1960s caused the NBA to focus on engaging the best talent, whatever their race and ethnicity. Freed from the constraints of a quota system, basketball benefitted from Black superstars like Kareem Abdul-Jabbar (debut 1969), Magic Johnson (debut 1979), and Michael Jordan (debut 1984). Far from upholding a color line that limited Black players, the NBA began to adopt Black culture, embracing hip-hop music and fashionable trainers while pushing ticket sales and merchandising to African Americans. The result was startling. By 2020, 74.2 percent of basketballers in the NBA were Black, the highest proportion in American professional sports leagues.

END ZONE

A similar story of spectacular growth in Black participation occurred in American football. The National Football League (NFL) had imposed an unofficial ban on Black players since 1934, another barrier imposed by White team owners, especially George Preston Marshall of the Washington Redskins. It was broken in 1946, a year before Jackie Robinson made his baseball debut, by the Los Angeles Rams, who were told they would be barred from using the city's publicly funded Coliseum stadium if they remained a segregated team. The Rams' management

The dropping of the unofficial race quota in basketball allowed Chicago Bulls to dominate the league in the 1980s and 1990s with stars like Dennis Rodman, Scottie Pippen, and Michael Jordan

The NFL's first Black players Woody Strode (27) and Kenny Washington (13) played alongside pioneer baseballer Jackie Robinson (28) on the 1939 UCLA football team

signed Kenny Washington and Woody Strode, plucking them from a Californian semi-professional football league.

The next couple of decades saw a steady increase in the number of Black footballers. By 1970, one third of players in the NFL were Black. By 2019, 58.9 percent of players identified as Black or African American. Among their predecessors were Joe Perry, the first Black player to be named the league's Most Valuable Player, Emlen Tunnell, the first Black player to be voted into the Hall of Fame, and Jim Brown, a three-time MVP.

RACIAL STEREOTYPES

Despite the increase in Black participation in the NFL, certain roles remained largely off limits until recently. For decades, Black players have dominated the positions that rely on speed – cornerback, running back, and wide receiver – but there have been few Black players at quarterback, the most important position that leads the offense. Stereotyping of players by race has been blamed. Studies show that scouting and media reports were likely to mention the athleticism of Black players, while White players were typically praised for their ability to study the game.

As a result, coaches slotted players into positions based on racial stereotypes. When

> "SOME BLACK SPORTS STARS HAVE USED THEIR MEDIA PLATFORMS TO DEMAND EQUALITY OFF THE FIELD"

Black quarterback Marlin Briscoe was drafted by the Denver Broncos in 1968, he fought to not be reassigned as a cornerback. Though players like Warren Moon and Randall Cunningham carved out successful careers in subsequent years, it was not until the 21st century that Black quarterbacks have become commonplace. In 2020, ten out of 32 starting quarterbacks were Black or multiracial. Four of them are among the five highest-paid players in the NFL.

If the unofficial color line that blocked Black footballers becoming quarterbacks has been breached, the one that stands between Black people and head coaching jobs in American football is stubbornly unbroken. The Rooney Rule was adopted by the NFL as a form of affirmative action, requiring teams to provide evidence that at least one ethnic-minority candidate had been interviewed for head coaching vacancies. However, the impact of the policy appears to have been minimal. At the beginning of the 2021 season there were three Black head coaches in the NFL, exactly the same number as there were when the Rooney Rule was instituted in 2003, and only one had been in post for more than two seasons.

TAKING A KNEE

While the lack of Black head coaches in the NFL suggests progress is still to be made, the general shift towards racial equality in sport is startling. So too is the growth in cultural influence that athletes wield, the result of television coverage, sponsorship, and social media. Some Black sports stars have used their vast salaries and media platforms to demand equality off the field.

In a preseason game before the 2016 NFL campaign began, San Francisco 49ers quarterback Colin Kaepernick chose to kneel during the playing of the national anthem to protest police brutality and the oppression of the Black community. He was subsequently joined by hundreds of players from across the NFL and other sports, including a handful of White players.

It was a controversial protest. President Donald Trump weighed in, saying that kneeling during the anthem was "a total disrespect of our heritage" and calling for kneeling players to be fired. Kaepernick was released by the 49ers at the end of the 2016 season (likely for footballing reasons) but he blamed his inability to land a spot with a new team on being blackballed by the NFL.

One sportsman too valuable to be blackballed was LeBron James, one of the most decorated basketballers in NBA history. He has also used his public platform to speak out on issues of racial equality. He persuaded his Miami Heat teammates to wear hoodies for a photoshoot to protest the shooting of Trayvon Martin in 2012 and appeared on court in a T-shirt referencing the death of Eric Garner in police custody in 2014. James's protests have drawn scorn from some political commentators, however, his activism has helped inspire basketball to respond to the fatal shootings of Black people by police officers with protests.

After the killing of Jacob Blake in August 2020, the Milwaukee Bucks refused to take the court for their playoff match against Orlando Magic. The NBA swiftly postponed all the matches due to take place that evening and the following day. Players in the Women's NBA had already dedicated the 2020 season to Breonna Taylor and female victims of police brutality, wearing Taylor's name on the back of their shirts and walking off the court as the national anthem played.

That African-American sports stars can use their platforms to influence the wider world is a sign of the progress that has been made in professional sports, if not in society. When Branch Rickey chose to sign Jackie Robinson to the Brooklyn Dodgers, he wanted a player with the strength of character to not fight back against discrimination. Modern-day Black sport stars, in contrast, see fighting back against discrimination as part of the responsibility that their huge influence brings.

Mike Tomlin of the Pittsburgh Steelers is one of the few successful Black NFL head coaches in the era of the Rooney Rule

LeBron James was the reigning NBA MVP in 2014 when he wore a black shirt with the last words of Eric Garner before he died in police custody

In 1960, six-year-old Ruby Bridges had to be escorted to and from school by US Marshalls after becoming the first African-American child to desegregate an all-White school in New Orleans

Years after the ruling, President Eisenhower had to send federal troops to Little Rock, Arkansas, to force the integration of nine Black students into a previously all-White school

BROWN V BOARD OF EDUCATION

Even after the Civil War came to an end, it took another century for the US to desegregate its schooling system, which was designed to perpetuate inequality

I n 1896, the United States' Black populace was dealt a crushing blow when the Supreme Court ruled it legal to racially segregate public facilities, so long as Black and White people enjoyed equal standards – giving rise to a series of laws known as the 'Jim Crow' laws. Of course, given the deep socioeconomic legacy of slavery and the enduring nationwide prejudice against Black people, this absurd 'separate-but-equal' principle ended up reinforcing inequality from the ground up, depriving Black Americans access to decent schooling.

However, by the 1950s, the National Association for the Advancement of Colored People (NAACP) stepped up its campaign to dismantle segregation in public schools, with a series of lawsuits in South Carolina, Virginia, and Delaware. These efforts culminated in the 1951 case of Oliver Brown versus the Board of Education of Topeka, Kansas, where a Black girl had been denied entry into an all-White elementary school, which was the closest to her home – and was instead enrolled in a segregated Black school, a bus ride away.

Despite acknowledging the "detrimental" impact segregation had on Black children, Kansas' District Court did nothing to change it. Undeterred, the NAACP rolled five cases together into one, making it Brown v Board of Education of Topeka, and brought it before the Supreme Court in 1952.

Bolstered by copious amounts of evidence and legal precedent, the NAACP's brilliant Legal Defense and Educational Fund head, Thurgood Marshall, was able to successfully secure a unanimous verdict against school segregation in 1954. That May, Chief Justice Earl Warren wrote that the separate-but-equal doctrine had no place in public education, and that segregated schools were "inherently unequal."

Having considered the vast gulf between White and Black schools, the Supreme Court ordered the desegregation of schools "with all due speed." However, because the Court failed to stipulate how exactly desegregation should be carried out, it would take some time for the landmark to become implemented across the country – resulting in incidents such as in 1957's Little Rock Nine saga, where President Eisenhower had to dispatch federal troops to force an Arkansas school to allow nine Black students to attend a previously all-White school.

Civil rights attorneys celebrate victory outside the US Supreme Court. For his heroic efforts, Thurgood Marshall (center) was later dubbed 'Mr Civil Rights', before going on to become the first Black Supreme Court member

THE MURDER THAT SHOCKED AMERICA

The horrifying lynching of Emmett Till by two White racists was an important catalyst for the American Civil Rights Movement

Mamie said of Emmett's open casket: "I wanted the world to see what they did to my baby"

Emmett Till could have had no idea that he would still be remembered more than 60 years after his death, or that he would be seen as in any way significant to an important cause. Tragically, his death was more significant than his short life.

Till was born on July 25, 1941. Essentially raised by a single mother, Mamie (a violent father and stepfather made sporadic appearances), he grew up in Chicago, but was fascinated by the stories of the old days in the Mississippi Delta he heard from his great-uncle Mose. In the summer of 1955, aged just 14, he made the fateful decision to visit the segregated South where his mother was raised. Mamie warned him that it was a far more racially charged environment than Chicago, and that he must be very careful how he conducted himself in White company. He promised his mother he would.

Till initially settled in well in Money, Mississippi, the town where Mose was a local preacher. Till made friends quickly among the children of the local sharecroppers, but after only three days of his vacation, the events that would lead to the violent end of his young life began to spiral. While his friends played in the street, he went to buy two cents' worth of bubble gum from the grocery shop that was owned by a White couple called Roy and Carolyn Bryant.

Carolyn was working alone at the time, and would claim that Till grabbed her and made lascivious suggestions – a story she retracted later in life. Other witnesses stated that Till did almost nothing to attract attention to himself. He may have whistled at Carolyn as he left the store, but even there, contradictory reports have suggested that the whistle may have been a technique he used to combat his stutter, or that he was simply trying to attract the attention of

Bryant and Milam's legal team tried to convince the jury that the body wasn't Till's, and that he was still alive somewhere

a friend playing checkers across the street.

Whatever the truth, the idea of a Black boy behaving in a familiar fashion towards a White woman was not one that could be tolerated in the racist South of the United States where lynchings were still relatively commonplace. When Roy Bryant learned of the altercation, he flew into a rage. Enlisting the help of his half-brother John William Milam, he began a search for Emmett Till, which three days later, led him to the home of Mose and his family. Bryant and

Mamie with Emmett's great-uncle Mose

Carolyn Bryant in court with her husband Roy and their two children. Carolyn admitted in later life that she'd lied about Emmett Till

Bryant and Milam looking relaxed during their trial

CAROLYN BRYANT'S CONFESSION

The truth is that Emmett Till did little more than whistle at Carolyn Bryant – and may even have been whistling at a friend across the street and not at her at all. But whatever her reasons, Bryant testified that he grabbed her, verbally threatened her, and made lewd insinuations about his history with White women.

It took more than 50 years, but Bryant eventually admitted that she'd lied. Interviewed by author Timothy B. Tyson for his book, *The Blood of Emmett Till*, she finally broke her silence in 2007. "That part is not true," she said of the list of accusations she initially came up with. "Nothing that boy did could ever justify what happened to him." She went on to say that she also felt "tender sorrow" for Emmett's mother Mamie, and that the white supremacist segregation of her youth was wrong, although it had seemed normal at the time.

While she expressed regret, however, she didn't go quite so far as to apologize. The interview went public in 2017. It's since been denied that Bryant disavowed her testimony, but Tyson stands by his version.

Following Emmett's murder, Mamie went on to become a prominent educator and civil rights activist

Mamie, Emmett's mother, addressing an anti-lynching rally

Milam then forced entry, and dragged Till out of the house to a waiting pickup truck.

They drove him to a barn in Drew, Mississippi, pistol-whipped him, brutally beat him, and eventually shot him in the head. They then weighted his body and threw it in the Tallahatchie River, where it surfaced on August 31.

Unlike previous similar murders, however, Till's grisly and unjust end would not go unremarked. Early as Till's death was in the history of the Civil Rights Movement, the times he was living in were nevertheless politically and racially charged enough for the events in Money and Drew to make headline news across the United States. This had much to do with the fact that Till hailed from Chicago rather than the South, and with Mamie's decision to display Emmett's mutilated and unrecognizable corpse in an open casket. Newspaper photographs of the body shocked the entire country. Decent citizens of all colors and creeds were repulsed by the

Emmett's body was so unrecognizable when it was pulled from the water that he was identified only by the silver ring he wore

murder. Bryant and Milam could expect little support for their crime.

Except, they were acquitted. Five days in a sweltering segregated courtroom with an all-White jury meant the pair received an easy ride in the dock. Despite the evidence against them, and the testimonies of several witnesses – Black people accusing Whites in court was a courageous act for the time – they walked from the courtroom free men. Some of the jurors later admitted that they didn't think the killing of a Black man was worth a custodial or capital sentence. Immune from being tried twice for the same crime (under the now-defunct 'double jeopardy' law), Bryant and Milam even admitted their guilt in a lucrative magazine interview not long afterwards. This act of hubris worked against them. Their infamy followed them wherever they tried to settle, and their businesses were boycotted and went bankrupt. After bleak lives marked by violence and

petty crime, Milam died in 1980 and Bryant in 1994.

Till, meanwhile, lived on in people's imaginations, his death serving as the spark that ignited the Civil Rights Movement in earnest. The date of Emmett's murder, August 28, was also the day in 1963 that Martin Luther King Jr. made his 'I Have a Dream' speech. And when the Reverend Jesse Jackson asked Rosa Parks why she refused to give up her bus seat to a White passenger that day in December 1955, she replied that she had considered moving to the back of the bus, but then "thought of Emmett Till" and decided she couldn't.

Emmett Till's grave in Illinois

© Getty

Parks later stated that if she had realized that James Blake was the driver, she would never have got on the bus

7053

"DESPITE THEIR FREEDOM, LIFE FOR A YOUNG BLACK FAMILY IN THE DEEP SOUTH WAS EXTREMELY HARSH"

Parks poses for a press image seated at the front of the bus, the space that was reserved for Whites only

ROSA PARKS: TIRED OF GIVING IN

A small act of defiance, caused by a community pushed too far, would be the catalyst for the nationwide Civil Rights Movement

When the Civil Rights Movement is mentioned, few people would fail to think of the woman who almost single-handedly kick-started the national movement: Rosa Parks. Many aspects of 1950s American society were strictly segregated and while Parks was not the first person who refused to obey the laws, she was the spark that lit the fire of civil rights throughout the land.

In what was just another day for Parks, riding home on the Montgomery city bus after work, she was asked to give up her designated seat to a White person. She refused, was arrested, and her court case gained the support of the local chapter of the National Association for the Advancement of Colored People (NAACP), who organized a citywide bus boycott that ran for 381 days. This nonviolent protest gained national coverage, acting as a catalyst to spread the Civil Rights Movement across the entire country, headed by the young Baptist minister, Dr. Martin Luther King Jr. To attribute this to the actions of a single person seems unfair but Parks' act of defiance is often seen as the straw that broke the camel's back. It was one injustice too far that inspired a large chunk of the US population to rise up and fight for equality.

Parks herself came from humble beginnings having been born in Tuskegee, a small town near the Alabama state capital Montgomery, on February 4, 1913. Her parents, Leona and James McCauley, a teacher and carpenter, valued education and were strong advocates of racial equality. Despite their freedom and strong views, life for a young Black family in the Deep South was extremely harsh. The Black community relied almost entirely on the White population for work, but the jobs were often menial and offered very little in the way of pay and perks.

Rosa grew up attending segregated schools, but was forced to drop out of high school at 16 to care for her sick grandmother and later her mother. She would return to school years later, encouraged by her husband, to gain her high school diploma. It is a testament to her will, and others sharing her plight, that despite her oppressive beginnings, she grew up with a great sense of self-worth. Those that knew her explained that she was softly spoken but carried with her a quiet strength and determination that saw her fight hard when challenged.

Parks found a job as a seamstress at a textile factory in Montgomery and in 1932, aged 19, married Raymond Parks. Raymond, lacking a formal education of his own, was actively involved in the NAACP and Rosa would soon become involved as well. Her actions on December 1, 1955 reflect her passion for the cause, as she was not just a person who decided

> Before Parks, a young Black woman was arrested, but her case was not pursued as she had an assault charge on the police report

not to give up her seat, but a committed activist working to better the lives of Black people in Alabama and throughout the United States.

The incident in December was, to many, a routine occurrence. Buses in Montgomery were segregated by color, with the front reserved for White people and the back for Black people. This meant that a Black person would need to pay for their ticket at the front of the bus, get off and walk to the back door to find a seat. The bus drivers held ultimate authority in their vehicles, being able to move the segregation line back and force any Black person to give up their seat in busy periods. Failure to do so would mean getting thrown off the bus and having the police called. Parks had already had a run-in with the driver, James Blake, a few years beforehand when Blake had driven off while Parks exited the bus to walk to the back doors.

Parks, who had just finished a long shift, was seated on the crowded bus but in a row with three other African-American passengers. When Blake noticed a White man standing he ordered Parks and the others to give up their seats. While only one seat was needed, the law stated that Whites and Blacks couldn't be seated in the same row. The four at first refused, to which Blake replied, "You'd better make it light on yourselves and let me have those seats". While the others complied, Parks would not budge, stating that as she was not in the White section she didn't think she should have to give up her seat. When remembering the incident in later life, Parks said: "When that White driver stepped back toward us, when he waved his hand and ordered us up and out of our seats, I felt a determination to cover my body like a quilt on a winter night". With steely resolve, Parks

Parks, and other members of the boycott, would receive death threats for their actions

Edgar Nixon played an instrumental role in the bus boycott and bailed Rosa Parks out of jail

Women of the Civil Rights Movement

Fannie Lou Hamer
Having faced brutal beatings in jail campaigning for equal rights, Hamer spoke candidly of her experiences live on air in 1964, prompting President Lyndon B. Johnson to organize an impromptu press conference to draw media coverage away from this embarrassing insight into racist America. Hamer spoke of her terrible experiences at the 1964 Democratic Convention.

Dorothy Height
President of the National Council for Negro Women for 40 years, Dorothy worked tirelessly to help low-income schools and provide for poor families. Her efforts led President Obama to describe her as the "godmother of the Civil Rights Movement" in 2010. Height is seen by many as one of the key figures of the Civil Rights Movement.

Daisy Bates
An iconic member of the civil rights campaign, Bates' most famous achievement was leading the Little Rock Nine to enrol in the Little Rock Central High School in 1957. After Little Rock, Bates worked tirelessly to improve living conditions in her poor community.

Septima Clark
With her work including securing equal pay for Black teachers, Septima Clark was dubbed the "mother of the movement" by Martin Luther King Jr. and had been fighting for equality since 1919. Clark would continue her work with the SCLC until her retirement in 1970.

Bernice Robinson
Robinson was a civil rights activist who recognized the importance of education in the fight for equality. She helped set up Citizenship Schools in South Carolina and worked with the SCLC across the South to teach adult reading skills to help Black Americans pass literacy tests in order to vote.

Diane Nash
As the founder of the Student Nonviolent Coordinating Committee (SNCC), Diane Nash was one of the most influential figures of the entire Civil Rights Movement. She helped organize sit-ins and the now legendary Freedom Riders. Nash worked tirelessly around Nashville and beyond to win equal rights and end segregation.

Parks became a figurehead for the Civil Rights Movement and continued to fight for equality throughout her life

The SCLC is still active today with Charles Steele Jr. the current president, a position previously held by Dr. King's daughter Bernice

refused to move an inch, forcing Blake to call his supervisor, asking for advice. The response was simple: "Well then, Jim, you do it, you got to exercise your powers and put her off, hear?" Parks was then arrested as she had technically broken the law by not giving up her seat. While she was being arrested, she asked the police officer a question: "Why do you push us around?" The question and response of "I don't know, but the law is the law," along with Parks' actions, are widely credited as one of the catalysts for the Civil Rights Movement in America.

She was held in the police station for violating chapter 6, section 11 of the Montgomery city code that dealt with segregation. She was bailed out that evening by the president of the local NAACP chapter, Edgar Nixon. Nixon saw an opportunity to use Parks' arrest to further their cause and immediately began planning a boycott of the city's buses that night. The next day, the city was saturated with newspaper ads and over 35,000 handbills, produced the night before, were distributed around Black neighborhoods. The boycott called for all African Americans to avoid using the buses until they were treated with the same level of respect as White passengers while on board, the segregated seating was removed and Black drivers were hired. The Montgomery Improvement Association (MIA) was formed to

spearhead the initiative and at its head was Dr. Martin Luther King Jr., a recent newcomer to Montgomery and the man who saw a chance to use Parks' case to take the struggle nationwide.

The first day of the boycott coincided with Parks' trial, where she was fined $14. Continuing for another 380 days, the boycott saw many Black people shun the bus in favor of using Black taxi companies, carpooling, or simply walking to work – with some people walking up to 20 miles a day. It soon began to have the desired effect as the bus company's profits slumped, leading to much of the fleet sitting idle for over a year. The successes were tempered by the backlash, however, as Black churches were burned and both King's and Nixon's houses were attacked. The authorities also tried to break the boycott through other means, with the taxi companies that took Black people to work having their insurance revoked and arrests made under antiquated anti-boycott laws.

These heavy-handed reactions did little to sway the MIA who went on the legal offensive. Only a year before, the Brown v Board of Education Supreme Court ruling had found that segregated schools were unconstitutional. Armed with this, their legal team sought to challenge the segregation laws for public transport. In June 1956 they were ruled unconstitutional and despite resistance the

> **Black taxi companies reduced their fares to the price of a bus ticket in support of the boycott**

FORMATION OF THE SCLC

The Southern Christian Leadership Conference (SCLC) was an organization born out of the success of the Montgomery Bus Boycott. Headed by Martin Luther King Jr., the group sought to capitalize on the victory in Alabama and advance the cause of civil rights in a nonviolent manner. Black communities in the South at this time were formed around the church, so having a minister as the figurehead was an obvious choice. King himself stated, "The SCLC is church orientated because of the very structure of the Negro community in the South."

Combining various smaller civil rights groups under one spiritual umbrella, the SCLC formed three main goals which would be the bedrock of the organization. The first was to encourage White Southerners to join their cause. Although a staggering amount of hate and vitriol was levelled against Blacks in the South, the SCLC believed that not all people harbored racist views. All Black people were also encouraged and asked to "seek justice and reject all injustice." The final and perhaps most important point for the group was a strict belief and adherence to nonviolent protest. The unofficial motto of the group became "not one hair of one head of one White person shall be harmed."

decision was upheld by the Supreme Court in November 1956. With the law on their side and both the bus company and city businesses suffering financial losses, the city had little choice but to end segregation on public transport. The boycott was formally ended on December 20, 1956.

Rosa Parks' resistance ignited one of the largest and most successful protests against racial segregation in the South. Its nonviolent means saw it gain national coverage and helped to send the struggle for civil rights nationwide.

THE LITTLE ROCK NINE

In Little Rock, Arkansas in 1957, nine Black students asserted their right to education in a racially mixed school. Their first day did not go smoothly

Along with the Montgomery Bus Boycott and the speeches of Martin Luther King Jr., one of the most resonant events of the African-American struggle for civil rights took place in Little Rock, Arkansas, in September 1957. In every other way, Central High School was unremarkable, but it became the site of a crucial test to Supreme Court legislation.

The beginnings of the story were in 1951, when 13 parents in Topeka, Kansas filed a lawsuit against their local board of education. In the Southern states of America at that time, racial segregation was mandated by law. The Topeka parents, with the encouragement and support of the National Association for the Advancement of Colored People (NAACP), called for the district to reverse this policy. The named plaintiff in the case was Oliver L. Brown, and the subsequent case was named Brown v Board of Education of Topeka. It turned out to be a landmark ruling: the US Supreme Court, taking the case along with other similar filings from South Carolina, Virginia, Washington, and Delaware, concluded in May 1954 that having separate schools for White and Black students was unconstitutional. It called for immediate desegregation and reintegration of Black pupils into all-White schools. Problematically, however, it suggested no procedure by which this might be achieved.

In Arkansas, as elsewhere in the South, the school board largely accepted the ruling, took advice from the NAACP, and began planning for gradual reintegration, beginning in 1957 with its high schools. Undeterred by the vocal opposition of segregationist groups the Mothers' League of Central High School and the Capital Citizens' Council, nine students registered to be Central's first Black students. They were Minnijean Brown, Elizabeth Eckford, Ernest Green, Thelma Mothershed, Melba Pattillo, Gloria Ray, Terrence Roberts, Jefferson Thomas, and Carlotta Walls. Their first day at school made national headlines, but not for the reasons they might have hoped. They arrived at the school gates to find state troopers pointing guns at them.

The Governor of Arkansas at the time was Orval Faubus. He was a Democrat who had actually gained office as a progressive candidate. By September of 1957, however, he was struggling in the polls, finding that he was being strongly challenged by opponents who thrived on stoking the prejudices of the local White voters. Apparently for reasons of self-interest then, Faubus sided with the segregationists of his constituency. On September 2, he announced that he would be utilizing the Arkansas National Guard to block the Nine's entry to Central High. He claimed that this was for their own protection, citing the possibility of violence if they were allowed to attend the school as planned.

The Nine did indeed encounter hostility other than that of the military: crowds of baying White protesters turned out to make sure that the Nine knew they were unwelcome. Eckford, who arrived separately from the other eight, underwent a particularly terrifying ordeal (left), surrounded, alone, by a hostile mob.

The events attracted national and international publicity, and after only three

> **President Bill Clinton awarded each of the Nine a Congressional Gold Medal in 1999 for outstanding service to the USA**

days of the standoff, President Dwight D. Eisenhower was personally involved, threatening Faubus that "the Federal Constitution will be upheld by me by every legal means at my command." Faced with the ire of the president of the United States (not to mention possible jail time), Faubus became understandably conciliatory. On September 14, he traveled to Newport, Rhode Island, for a private conference with Eisenhower, the outcome of which saw Faubus agree to put aside his apparent personal views on segregation to comply with the Supreme Court's ruling. By September 21, Eisenhower was able to release a statement confirming that the Governor was withdrawing his troops, and the Nine would be welcomed unopposed to Central High, with officers of the local law ensuring their safety.

But even then, the matter wasn't settled. Two days later, likely with the tacit approval of Faubus, another organized mob formed outside the school, of such a size that the police could not control it. Genuinely for their own safety this time, the Nine were sent home once again. Eisenhower removed the Arkansas National Guard from Faubus's control, and replaced them with troops from the 101st Airborne Division to enforce federal law. The Nine attended their first day of classes on September 25.

Legal challenges to integration in Arkansas continued, however, and the Nine faced appalling hostility within Central High's walls: burned in effigy and on the receiving end of constant violent attacks. Brown retaliated, and was expelled for doing so. Green was ultimately the only one of the Nine to stick it out at Central High until graduation, although they all went on to distinguished careers. Green and Brown both went into politics, while Pattillo became a news reporter and broadcaster. The Nine all received personal invitations to attend President Barack Obama's inauguration ceremony in 2009.

> **Central High School still exists, and is now a historic site also housing a civil rights museum**

LITTLE ROCK'S 'LOST YEAR'

Orval Faubus was not going to take interference in his state lightly, even from the US President himself. Despite apparently convivial talks intended to help diffuse the situation in Little Rock, the White protests against the Black students were thought to be ongoing with Faubus's tacit – if not public – approval. And when Eisenhower sent in troops to decisively enforce federal law, Faubus took the extraordinary measure of shutting down all of Little Rock's high schools for the school year of 1958-59. The period has become known as Little Rock's 'Lost Year'.

Faubus's reasoning was that the imposition of federal troops beyond his control on Little Rock was a usurpation of power by central government. The peculiar situation saw teachers continuing to show up for work in empty classrooms while students of all races were barred from attending – although sports fixtures like football games were allowed to continue. Some students went to school in neighboring counties, some went to work or joined the military, and many simply dropped out.

The Lost Year ended in June 1959, when federal courts declared the closures, like segregation, were unconstitutional. Public high schools reopened on August 12, 1959, with desegregation continuing slowly and Black students still facing considerable discrimination.

Governor Orval E. Faubus

AMERICA GOT SOUL

Founded on the marriage of spirituality and sexuality, soul grew into one of America's most powerful art forms, becoming forever ingrained in the nation's cultural identity

Soul is a broad tree, with roots stretching deep into the heart of the African-American experience. It can be traced all the way back to the earliest Afro-American music – gospel and blues – two spiritual accompaniments to the lives of hardship that Black people experienced from the earliest days of slavery, right through to the Jim Crow era. While gospel emerged as a source of hope for a brighter tomorrow, even if one had to wait for the afterlife to enjoy it, blues was a direct product of slavery and prejudice; a cathartic outpouring of the misery, hardship, and pain so intertwined with the lives of America's viciously oppressed underclass.

Blues had once been played exclusively in the smoky, sweaty Black drinking establishments dotted along the Mississippi Delta. There, virtuosos like Robert Johnson stunned audiences by hurtling their sweaty fingers across guitars with remarkable musical proficiency, and stunning emotional depth. However, as more Black people migrated to seek opportunities in new cities, the genre soon traveled to hubs such as Chicago, where it adapted to the miseries resulting from urban poverty. There it took on a new life, as once acoustic musicians like Muddy Waters went electric, playing in booming bars for dancing audiences.

Simultaneously, other Black musicians had taken traditions into an entirely new direction; pioneering the genre of jazz, featuring large brass bands and syncopated rhythms. Musicians like Louis Armstrong gradually took White America by storm, to the point that White people began to appropriate this new genre for itself; 'legitimizing' it in the eyes of the White establishment. The genre's success paved the way for 'race' music to begin building an infrastructure and industry, owned and maintained by Black entrepreneurs, for Black artists; training an entire generation of musicians, producers, songwriters, engineers, and talent. Even White rock bands were now heavily inspired by Black music, which had made the White crooners of yesteryear utterly redundant.

> "WHITE PEOPLE BEGAN TO APPROPRIATE THIS NEW GENRE FOR ITSELF; 'LEGITIMIZING' IT"

FOOD FOR THE SOUL

During the 1950s, a new generation of post-war musicians began to bring together the rapidly developing forms of Black music, merging the melodies of gospel revival with the upbeat articulation of doo-wop and rhythm and blues, giving rise to an entirely new genre; soul. This new style was personified in the forms of the upcoming musicians Ray Charles and Sam Cooke, ushering in a new popular, secular artform.

Emerging from Los Angeles, the blind Ray Charles took his influences from Charles Brown and Nat King Cole into the stratosphere, bursting out jazz-blues-gospel hybrid hits such as 1959's 'What'd I Say', before becoming one of the first Black crossover artists with Hoagy Carmichael's 'Georgia on My Mind', and Percy Mayfield's

Marvin Gaye helped to shape the Motown Sound throughout the 1960s and in 1971 he released the ground-breaking album, What's Going On

barnburner, 'Hit the Road Jack'. Black musician Bobby Womack later commented, "Ray was the genius. He turned the world onto soul music." *Billboard* magazine writer Jerry Wexler even coined a new term for 'race music'; dubbing it 'rhythm and blues'.

Charles had done the seemingly impossible, bridging the sexual energy of the dancefloor and the spiritual energy of the church. Charles's 'What'd I Say' was considered so obscene that it was banned in some parts of the country; even being described as "sacrilegious" by some, for secularizing gospel music, and adding a touch of innuendo. And despite breaking through to White America, the 'Queen of R&B' Ruth Brown recalled, "When the dance was over sometimes it was so scary we wanted to get out of town as soon as we could. There were still crosses burning in the middle of the night. There was a price paid for this music."

GETTING IN ON THE ACTION

For a while, Black musicians such as Little Richard and Chuck Berry had revolutionised the face of popular culture; and showed up the country's White musicians in the process. However, artists once again began to push Black musicians out, by appropriating the increasingly popular rock 'n' roll genre, which Charles differentiated as: "Rock 'n' roll is the White version of rhythm and blues. There was a big difference, if you really listened to the music, between the two styles. One is more pure, one is more dirty. R&B has got more toe jam in it." In response, he returned to his roots, "I started taking my music and saying it the way that I felt

Among Motown's best-selling groups of the 1960s, Martha Reeves and the Vandellas were inducted into the Rock and Roll Hall of Fame in 1995

it – the gospel sound that was part of my growing up. I knew all I was doing was being myself."

Meanwhile, after a string of hits with the Soul Stirrers, including 'Be With Me Jesus' and 'Touch the Hem of His Garment', the Chicago-raised Sam Cooke soared to new heights with Bump Blackwell's 1957 tune, 'You Send Me'. Selling more than a million copies, 'You Send Me' was a

defining moment; inspiring a whole generation of Black musicians. For many, the world of soul is marked by life before 1957, and life after it. Music writer Peter Guralnick explains, "You couldn't have the popular music we have today without that crossover from church to pop." With the Soul Stirrers, Cooke toured a network of Black churches called the 'gospel highway' for seven years. It was a jarring life; treated as a superstar in one breath, and dealing with dangerous racism the next. Bobby Womack remembers, "Sam was electrifying. The places were jam-packed – it was like Elvis Presley was coming." Sam Cooke's crossover success was a milestone in the marriage of gospel, rhythm and blues, and rock 'n' roll. While Ray Charles tore his way through his songs, Cooke crooned through a clean tenor voice, establishing himself as a genre mainstay, as it transitioned into the more socially conscious 1960s.

COMING TO THE FORE

As the Civil Rights Movement swelled, so too did the Black pride movement; and this soon began to trickle out into culture and entertainment. While The Staple Singers inspired a young Bob Dylan, the charts themselves were taken over by Berry Gordy's Black-run Detroit record label, Motown. Soul groups like The Supremes, The Miracles, Martha and the Vandellas, and the Four Tops dominated the charts with their powerful lead vocals, set against beautiful harmonies, big brass sections, rich arrangements, and luxurious melodies.

However, amid the changing tides, Motown momentarily found itself out of touch with the

SOUL'S FORGOTTEN SUPERSTAR

With his stratospheric voice weighed down by mental health issues, James Carr's career was def ined as much by what it was as what it should have been

James Carr's soaring voice was weighed down by his struggles with mental health

One of soul's finest singers is ironically one of its least known. Born in 1942, Carr grew up in Memphis, and cut his teeth singing with a variety of gospel groups throughout the 1960s. Having failed to find success in Memphis, he released his first single 'You've Got My Mind Messed Up' with the entrepreneurial producer, Quinton Claunch. His follow-up, 'Dark End of the Street' became an instant classic, covered by everyone from Aretha Franklin to Linda Ronstadt – none of whom ever rose to the heights of Carr's raw emotion and earth-shaking performance.

A shy man who suffered with mental illness,

what Carr lacked in charisma he more than made up for in extraordinary vocals; able to catapult from a roaring deep baritone to a shrill shriek in an instant, never missing a note or beat. Although he was largely absent during the 1970s and 1980s, he had a brief comeback in the 1990s with two records, before dying in 2001, leaving behind five children. Years earlier, when the singer Dan Penn was touring the UK, he commented, "Everybody keeps asking me which is my favorite version of 'Dark End of the Street' – as if there was any other than James Carr's. Not even mine. I'll sing it anyway. But I wish I had James here."

Sam Cooke's crossover success was a milestone; one he followed by setting up his own record label, and aligning the genre with the Civil Rights Movement

pulse of America. Instead, it was up to Chicago's Renaissance man, Curtis Mayfield, to tap into the public sentiment. Having already established himself as a singer, guitarist, songwriter and arranger, he began to write about community struggle and racial harmony. His 1964 track, 'People Get Ready', held up a mirror to the zeitgeist of the time, "People get ready, there's a train a comin'/You don't need no baggage, you just get on board/All you need is faith to hear the diesel's hummin'/ You don't need no ticket, you just thank the lord" – later going on to inspire Bob Marley's 'One Love/ People Get Ready'. Mayfield explained, "That was taken from my church or from the upbringing of messages from the church. Like there's no hiding place and get on board, and images of that sort. I must have been in a very deep mood of that type of religious inspiration when I wrote that song."

> "THROUGHOUT THE 1960S, AMERICA'S SOUL ACTS CONTINUED TO INNOVATE, BECOMING MORE POLITICAL"

As the genre grew increasingly popular among White audiences and musicians, it gave way to a new genre dubbed 'Blue-eyed soul' – soul music performed by White people. Music magazines applied the term to White acts such as the Righteous Brothers, Tom Jones, and husband and wife duo, Sonny & Cher. While some Black stations initially refused to play these acts, some were able to break through; distinguishing themselves from White performers who simply 'stole' Black music, by carefully devoting themselves to studying and faithfully replicating the Black genre.

Throughout the 1960s, America's soul acts continued to innovate, becoming increasingly political. This newfound purpose fuelled Sam Cooke's poignant 1964 song, 'A Change is Gonna Come', which immediately became an anthem of the Civil Rights Movement, as it headed into its peak. Cooke

was inspired firstly by an incident when a hotel clerk turned him and his wife away for being Black, and secondly by Bob Dylan's 'Blowin' in the Wind', which in turn drew its melody and concept from the old Black spiritual, 'No More Auction Block/We Shall Overcome'. Just two weeks before the song's release, Cooke was murdered in a Los Angeles motel, his words reverberating forevermore as a call for justice

Curtis Mayfield provided the soundtrack to the film Super Fly; an astute embodiment of the reality of life in the ghetto

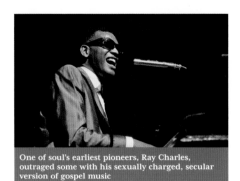

One of soul's earliest pioneers, Ray Charles, outraged some with his sexually charged, secular version of gospel music

In 1967, Aretha Franklin forever changed the male-dominated face of soul with a sensational string of hits

and equality. By the time of his death, Cooke had amassed 30 Top 40 singles, blazing a trail by forming his own publishing company and record label years before that was commonplace for Black musicians. He was also among the first to forgo a slick flattened 'conk' hairstyle, in favor of an Afro. Together with Motown's Gordy, he had helped transition the industry into a vehicle for political change, by helping to cross over the picket lines of racism, breaking into venues and radio stations previously reserved for White acts.

FEMALE FORCE

Born in Memphis and raised in Detroit, Aretha Franklin began her singing career in her father's church, where she caught the attention of John Hammond from Columbia Records – the same man who discovered a young Bob Dylan. After recording ten albums in six years, she grew frustrated and moved to Atlantic Records, where her career finally blossomed. Until the mid-1960s, the genre was dominated by male superstars. However, all that changed in 1967, when Franklin scored a stunning series of hits, including 'I Never Loved a Man (The Way I Love You)', 'Do Right Woman, Do Right Man', 'Chain of Fools', 'Baby I Love You', '(You Make Me Feel Like) A Natural Woman', and the classic Otis Redding track, 'Respect'. Franklin's seminal 'I Never Loved a Man (The Way I Love You)' was recorded at producer Rick Hall's Fame Studios in Muscle Shoals, Alabama – the same place another legendary lady, Etta James, recorded 'Tell Mama' and 'I'd Rather Go Blind'.

By the late 1960s, the genre had begun to form a series of subgenres. Under the vision of Motown songwriters Norman Whitfield and Barrett Strong, The Temptations started producing increasingly psychedelic soul. These tracks featured distorted guitars, multi-tracked drums, and elaborate vocal arrangements, flowing across longer, more experimental structures. Originally recorded by The Undisputed Truth, The Temptations' version of the Whitfield-Strong track 'Papa Was a Rollin' Stone' became a sensation, earning a Grammy. Meanwhile, another of Motown's rising stars, Marvin Gaye, embodied the tumultuous spirit of the 1970s with his masterpiece, *What's Going On*, a concept album about a veteran of the Vietnam War returning to an America riddled by hatred,

Another of soul's blind virtuosos, Stevie Wonder stunned listeners with the dizzyingly creative, and immaculately written 1973 record, Innervisions

Thundering across the stage to hypnotic rhythms and blasts of brass, James Brown was soon known as the 'Godfather of Soul' and 'Hardest Working Man in Show Business'

Inspired by acid culture and science fiction, George Clinton pioneered a distinct brand of funk, which went on to inspire some of rap's most iconic producers decades later

poverty, and injustice. It is considered not just one of the finest soul albums, but one of the greatest records of all time.

By this time, Georgia singing sensation James Brown had pioneered his own unique sound; spearheaded by a masterful band including the innovative guitarist Jimmy Nolan, Alfred 'Pee Wee' Ellis on alto sax, Maceo Parker on tenor sax, Fred Wesley on trombone, and the stratospheric Bootsy Collins on bass. As he screamed and wailed his way through thumping tunes, clad in a sparkly, tight jumpsuit, Brown dripped head to toe with sweat, energy, and sexuality. From 'Please Please Please' (1956), through to 'Papa's Got a Brand New Bag' (1965), and 'Say It Loud, I'm Black and I'm Proud' (1968), he had grown increasingly confident in his own direction. By the 1970s, he stood at the forefront of an entirely new genre; funk. Characterized by repetitive rhythmic sections, with an emphasis on groove, Brown's tracks were entrancing, hypnotic powerhouses; with sections punctuated by wild, immaculately coordinated brass-blasting breakdowns.

He was joined in this genre by former Motown songwriter George Clinton, who went on to create the bands Parliament and Funkadelic; bringing together the styles of James Brown, Jimi Hendrix, Frank Zappa, and fellow funk pioneers, Sly and the Family Stone. Bootsy Collins would later go on to join the ensemble, who pioneered their own subgenre of P-Funk. If James Brown was drenched in sexuality, P-Funk was ablaze with cosmic, psychedelic creativity, with the band performing elaborate stage shows inspired by acid culture and science fiction. Decades

later, Clinton's music would become a staple of the emerging hip hop genre, as his songs were sampled by everyone from MC Hammer to Snoop Dogg – inspiring the G-Funk genre heralded by Digital Underground, Dr. Dre, and Warren G.

By the end of the 1970s, the smooth sound of Philadelphia soul's frontrunners, the Bluenotes, Delfonics, and O'Jays had paved the way for a new genre. The broad strings and sharp bass, famously produced by Kenny Gamble and Leon Huff, gave rise to disco;

emerging from the Black, Latino, and gay communities in the New York area. Before long, it took the nation by storm, immortalized in the hit film, *Saturday Night Fever*. While music was set on a new traje ctory, soul continued to endure; not just through the hip hop and R&B genres of the 1990s and 2000s, but also neo-soul revival acts, such as the late Sharon Jones and Charles Bradley, and Nashville's Robert Finley and Shannon Shaw; becoming ingrained within the very DNA of popular music.

Among the most unexpected offshoots of soul was disco, heralded by New York's Black, Latino, and gay communities

© Alamy, Getty

SIT-INS AND FREEDOM RIDES

As the Civil Rights Movement gathered pace, peaceful protestors devised a set of ingenious forms of peaceful protest, exposing the harsh reality of racism in America

n 1958, a group of 13 Black students and their teacher did the unfathomable; they walked into a major Oklahoma City drugstore and sat down, waiting to be seated. At the time, the city's lunch counters were still segregated by race, and this was considered a major taboo. Remarkably, when asked to leave, the group politely refused. And as racists began spitting at them and pummeling them with punches and kicks, they quietly refused to yield. After two days of abuse, one of the store's employees relented and handed one of the children a hamburger. That was all it took.

Two years later, on February 1, four Black college students entered a Whites-only lunch counter at a local store in North Carolina and ordered coffee. Despite being refused, threatened, and intimidated, they remained and simply waited to be served. Within days, they were joined by 300 students, whose presence effectively shut down the entire lunch counter. With heavy media attention fixed on the event, it grew into a national phenomenon, inspiring a wave of 'sit-ins' across the country, dismantling the system of racial discrimination one outlet at a time, as each quietly integrated their services.

However, there was more work to be done. Although the Supreme Court had already ruled it illegal to segregate interstate travel services, in practice, this had yet to be tested. When a group of Black Freedom Riders decided to see what happened when they boarded buses already carrying White people in Alabama on Mother's Day 1961, they too were attacked, with White racists hurling rocks, bricks, and firebombs at them. Later, some Black and White passengers were battered bloody when they strolled into segregated bus terminals together. Over the ensuing year, 400 volunteers, trained in nonviolence, enrolled in the Freedom Riders, traveling across the South to draw attention to the inequality and segregation that still plagued much of the country.

These forms of peaceful protest were instrumental in building momentum and support for the wider Civil Rights Movement, culminating in the monumental Civil Rights Act of 1964, which would eradicate institutional segregation once and for all.

The sit-ins were a brilliant form of peaceful protest; one that rapidly exposed, and dismantled, the fault-lines of America's archaic system of segregation

Among the original Freedom Riders was civil rights leader John Lewis, who was assaulted and arrested for exercising his rights

POLICE DEPT.
JACKSON, MISS
20886
5-24-61

A Greyhound bus used by the Freedom Riders is set on fire by White racists after arriving in Anniston, Alabama, in May 1961

THE CAMPAIGN THAT CHANGED AMERICA

In the most segregated city in America, the civil rights campaign met opposition that would not back down. The confrontation would come to define the movement

Many attempts were made to intimidate Reverend Shuttlesworth, but he refused to back down on his demands

"THE CITY GOVERNMENT WAS FIRMLY COMMITTED TO RACIAL SEGREGATION"

Black protesters kneel before city hall, Birmingham, Alabama, minutes before being arrested for parading without a permit, April 6, 1963

P rior to the Birmingham Campaign, the Civil Rights Movement had begun to flounder in the face of Black apathy and White indifference. The Albany Movement of late 1961 and 1962 had largely failed in the face of careful policing that employed the movement's own principle of nonviolence. But after the Birmingham Campaign, what had been a largely ignored regional protest commanded national and international attention. The city of Birmingham, Alabama, was where everything changed.

In 1963, Birmingham was one of the most segregated cities in the United States. Although the population was 40 percent Black, no Black people were employed in department stores, as bus drivers, or worked for the fire department or police force. The only employment available to them, outside of Black neighborhoods, was manual labor or working as a house servant. The city's downtown shopping area was also rigidly segregated, with 'whites-only' counters and toilets, separate circles for Black people in movie theaters, and so on. The city government was firmly committed to racial segregation: when the courts overturned the requirement that the city's parks be segregated, the city authorities closed the parks.

It was against this background that Reverend Fred Shuttlesworth, pastor of the Bethel Baptist Church from 1953 to 1961, asked the Southern Christian Leadership Conference (SCLC) to come to Birmingham to help the boycott he was organizing locally against segregated businesses. As Shuttlesworth said, "If you win in Birmingham, as Birmingham goes, so goes the nation."

The joint campaign began on April 3, 1963 with sit-ins at downtown whites-only lunch counters. Martin Luther King Jr. and the SCLC had learned from past mistakes to narrow their aims: rather than desegregate the whole city, they wanted to apply economic boycotts and nonviolent protests at the city's downtown businesses in the hope that local businessmen would then persuade the city authorities to change their opposition to desegregation. To that end, they organized an economic boycott of downtown businesses and, in response, some business owners began taking down their 'white only' notices. However, the city authorities, and in particular the Commissioner for Public Safety, Eugene 'Bull' Connor, fought back, cutting a food program and warning businesses that had desegregated that they would lose their licenses to trade.

The SCLC knew that they needed to gain national attention for their campaign and, in

© Getty

THE LETTER FROM A JAIL CELL

While he was being held in solitary confinement in jail, Martin Luther King Jr. read a copy of a newspaper, dated April 12, which contained an open letter from eight white clergymen, entitled 'A Call for Unity', which criticized protests "directed and led in part by outsiders." King formulated a reply, writing first on the margins of the paper, then on scraps of paper and finally finished on a pad supplied by his lawyer. The reply, which became known as the 'Letter from Birmingham Jail', sought to explain and justify the principles and practice of nonviolent protest in the face of entrenched injustice – it is King's longest and most sustained exploration of the beliefs that motivated him and the way in which he sought to apply them. To answer the charge that he was an outsider stirring trouble in Birmingham, King wrote that he had been invited to join the protests and that "injustice anywhere is a threat to justice everywhere. We are caught in an inescapable network of mutuality, tied in a single garment of destiny. Whatever affects one directly, affects all indirectly." To answer the charge that he was an extremist, King pointed out that Jesus himself had been seen as an extremist. "So the question is not whether we will be extremists, but what kind of extremists we will be. Will we be extremists for hate or for love?" King's colleagues edited together the letter as it was smuggled out to them, and portions of it were published on May 19, 1963 in the New York Post Sunday Magazine.

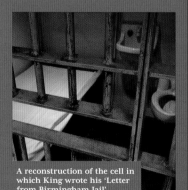
A reconstruction of the cell in which King wrote his 'Letter from Birmingham Jail'

'Bull' Connor, they were confident they had found the man who would bring them that attention. A dedicated segregationist, Connor was not a man to back down from a fight. When Klansmen beat up Freedom Riders in 1961, Connor made sure the police didn't arrive until the perpetrators had escaped. As he said to the press, "[W]e are not going to stand for this in Birmingham. And if necessary we will fill the jail full and we don't care whose toes we step on."

That was what King and the SCLC were counting on. They increased the nonviolent protests, with marches, kneel-ins at segregated churches, and sit-ins at libraries and lunch counters. The aim was to fill the city's jails with so many protestors that the governmental machinery would grind to a halt. But much of the local Black community was apathetic, while sections of local Black leadership were openly hostile, convinced that the campaign would only inflame passions when Connor was due to retire from office soon.

'Bull' Connor unwittingly did more to advance Black civil rights than most people

On April 10, the city authorities obtained a court order against the protests and began arresting protesters. The protest leaders decided to defy the injunction, but they were running

desperately short of funds with which to bail the arrested campaigners. Some of the other leaders suggested that Martin Luther King Jr., as the main fundraiser for the campaign, should leave Birmingham to tour the country raising funds so that bail could be posted and those arrested, released. After prayer alone in his room, King said, "I don't know what will happen; I don't know where the money will come from. But I have to make a faith act."

On April 12, Good Friday 1963, King led a protest march and was arrested and held in solitary confinement. While in jail, he wrote his famous 'Letter from Birmingham Jail'. King was held in prison until April 20.

The arrest (his 13th) and imprisonment of Martin Luther King Jr. had drawn national attention and even the president, John F. Kennedy, had become involved. But to maintain the attention, the SCLC had to increase the pressure on the city's authorities. To that end, they decided to up the stakes, and offer the most innocent members of their movement as agents of nonviolent protest: the children would march.

James Bevel, an SCLC organizer, had proposed the idea and, after much hesitation, King had approved it. Many local Black families were wary of the economic consequences of losing the family breadwinner to jail if they took part in the protests. But Bevel was confident that local students were

When King was arrested, his wife, Coretta, had just given birth to their fourth child, Bernice

"STUDENTS WERE READY AND WILLING TO TAKE ON THE MANTLE OF NONVIOLENT PROTEST"

African-American children are attacked by dogs and water cannons during a protest against segregation

ready and willing to take on the mantle of nonviolent protest, particularly after he ran workshops for them, including how to overcome the all-too-real fear of police dogs. Soon, these students would face these fears for real.

On May 2, over a thousand young Black people who had congregated at the 16th Street Baptist Church, began a march, a 'Children's Crusade', into downtown Birmingham in defiance of the city authorities and court injunctions. 'Bull' Connor was caught off guard by the size of the protest, and ordered the police to make mass arrests: over 600 were taken to jail. The city's jails were now overflowing.

What was more, national media had gathered in Birmingham to cover the events. A more level-headed man might have taken note of this, but not Connor. When, the next day, another thousand young people began to march towards the downtown, Connor ordered water cannons be turned on the marchers. These were high-pressure hoses, powerful enough to knock people flying and flay skin from flesh. Then, when bystanders called out against these tactics, Connor ordered that police dogs be sent in. The waiting photographers captured searing images of German shepherd dogs attacking young Black people who, true to the principles of nonviolence, made no move to protect themselves, while reporters wired stories of the unrest to the national press. Birmingham had become front-page news.

Seeing the way their children had been treated, the local Black community rallied behind the protests, which continued during the following week until the jails were so full that the enclosures at the state fairground were turned into holding pens. Business in downtown Birmingham came to a complete halt. On May 8, business leaders agreed to desegregate. And on May 10, the city authorities finally caved in, agreeing to bring an end to segregated toilets, drinking fountains, and lunch counters, the release on bail of the protesters held in jail, and a plan to increase Black employment.

The response from die-hard segregationists was violent, including bombs aimed at killing King, and in reality, the city authorities dragged their feet in implementing the agreement. But the Birmingham Campaign had succeeded in convincing President Kennedy that civil rights could no longer be left at state level. On June 11, 1963, he called for legislation to protect the rights of every American, regardless of race or religion. This would become the Civil Rights Act of 1964, the landmark legislation that outlawed discrimination, and it was signed into law by President Lyndon Johnson on July 2, 1964. The Birmingham Campaign had triumphed.

African-American protesters, seen through a paddy wagon window, sing and pray during a protest at Birmingham Jail

> Speaking to his wife from jail, King was careful in what he said, fearing the phone was bugged

The mugshot of Martin Luther King Jr. taken after his arrest on April 12

On May 11, segregationists planted a bomb in the motel where King and other leaders of the SCLC had been staying

THE MAKING OF AN ICON

The single most iconic photograph of the Birmingham protests, run across three columns on the front page of the New York Times on May 4, 1963, shows a young Black lad being attacked by a vicious police dog as a police officer holds the boy immobile. The boy himself, in an attitude of calm indifference, seems to personify the ideals of nonviolent protest. That's what the photo appears to show. But it

The iconic image of the Birmingham Campaign is not quite what it seems

turns out that the photo was not what it seemed. The boy in the photo, Walter Gadsden, wasn't even part of the protest but had bunked school and wanted to see what was going on. Moreover, Gadsden, when interviewed, has stated that rather than the police officer attacking him, he was trying to hold the dog back. When Gadsden's parents saw the picture in the paper the next day, they were appalled that their son had cut class. Gadsden was, nevertheless, arrested: the photo, taken by Bill Hudson, made him the unwitting face of the Birmingham Campaign.

"I HAVE A DREAM"

Explore the blood, sweat, and tears behind one of the most iconic speeches in American history

Martin Luther King Jr., the pastor who believed in nonviolent protest, addressed the hundreds of thousands of people gathered in Washington, D.C. with these words: "I am happy to join with you today in what will go down in history as the greatest demonstration for freedom in the history of our nation." The date was August 28, 1963 and while he spoke confidently, no one really knew how significant his role and the words he was yet to speak, sharing his iconic dream, would be in bringing it to life.

The day's events – known officially as The March on Washington for Jobs and Freedom – had been in planning since December 1962. An original focus on unemployment among the Black population had swiftly expanded to include the broader issue of segregation and discrimination, and soon a program of speeches, song and prayer had been arranged, reflecting a powerful vision of racial equality. Dr. Martin Luther King Jr. – the man now synonymous with the march and arguably Black history itself – was last on the bill.

Proceedings started early. Word of the march had spread far and wide, and at 8 a.m. the first of 21 chartered trains arrived in the capital, followed by more than 2,000 buses and ten airplanes – all in addition to standard scheduled public transport. Around 1,000 people – Black and White – poured into Lincoln Memorial every five minutes, including a number of well-known celebrities, which gave the march extra visibility. Charlton Heston and Burt Lancaster were among

King gave his speech to just under a quarter of a million people

GANDHI'S INFLUENCE

While the two never met, King derived a great deal of inspiration from Mahatma Gandhi's success in nonviolent protest, and so in 1959, made the journey to Bombay (now Mumbai).

King and his entourage were greeted with a warm welcome: "Virtually every door was open to us," King later recorded. He noted that Indian people "love to listen to the Negro spirituals," and so his wife, Coretta, ended up singing to crowds as often as King lectured.

The trip affected King deeply. In a radio broadcast made on his last night in India, he said: "Since being in India, I am more convinced than ever before that the method of nonviolent resistance is the most potent weapon available to oppressed people in their struggle for justice and human dignity."

the demonstrators, as was Marlon Brando, brandishing an electric cattle prod – a less-than-subtle symbol of police brutality. Soon speakers were preparing to give their speeches to an audience of a quarter of a million, a far greater number than the 100,000 hoped for.

The growing crowd buzzed with hope and optimism, but undercurrents of unease also rippled through the throng. Against a backdrop of violent civil rights protests elsewhere around the country, President Kennedy had been reluctant to allow the march to go ahead, fearing an atmosphere of unrest. Despite the organizers' promise of a peaceful protest, the Pentagon had readied thousands of troops in the suburbs and nearly 6,000 police officers patrolled the area. Liquor sales were banned throughout the city, hospitals stockpiled blood plasma and cancelled elective surgeries, and prisoners were moved to other facilities – measures taken to prepare for the civil disobedience many thought an inevitable consequence of the largest march of its kind in US history.

Many of those attending the march feared

for their own safety but turned up on that warm August day because of how important they believed it was for their country, which was being ripped apart at the seams by race. In his book, *Like a Mighty Stream*, Patrik Henry Bass reported that demonstrator John Marshall Kilimanjaro, who traveled to the march from Greensboro, North Carolina, said that many attending the march felt afraid: "We didn't know what we would meet. There was no precedent. Sitting across from me was a Black preacher with a white collar. We talked. Every now and then, people on the bus sang 'Oh Freedom' and 'We Shall Overcome', but for the most part there wasn't a whole bunch of singing. We were secretly praying that nothing violent happened."

Kilimanjaro traveled over 300 miles to attend the march. Many from Birmingham, Alabama – where King was a particularly prominent figure – traveled for more than 20 hours by bus, covering 750 miles. Attendees had invested a great deal of time, money, and hope in the march, and anticipation – nervous or otherwise – was high.

The long road to civil rights in America

1619
● **First known slaves**
The first known instance of African slavery in the fledgling English Colonial America is recorded.

1712
● **New York Slave Revolt**
A group of 23 enslaved Africans kill nine White people. More than 70 Blacks are arrested and 21 subsequently executed. After the uprising, the laws governing Black people are made more restrictive.

1780
● **A minor victory**
Pennsylvania becomes the first state in the newly formed United States to abolish slavery by law.

1790-1810
● **Manumission of slaves**
Slaveholders in the upper South free their slaves following the revolution, and the percentage of free Blacks rises from one percent to ten percent.

1863
● **The Emancipation Proclamation**
President Abraham Lincoln proclaims the freedom of Blacks still in slavery across ten states – around 3.1 million people.

1865
● **Black Codes**
Black Codes are passed across the United States – but most notoriously in the South – restricting the freedom of Black people and condemning them to low-paid labor.

The headline speaker, Martin Luther King Jr., prominent activist, revered pastor, and diligent president of the Southern Christian Leadership Conference (SCLC) had yet to finalize his speech, despite retiring to bed at 4 a.m. the previous night after a long and wearied debate with his advisors. "The logistical preparations for the march were so burdensome that the speech was not a priority for us," King's confidante and speechwriter Clarence B. Jones has since admitted.

It wasn't until the evening before the march that seven individuals, including Jones, gathered together with King to give their input on the final remarks. It was Jones's job to take notes and turn them into a powerful address that would captivate the hearts and minds of the nation – no mean feat as everyone at the meeting had a significant stake in the speech and wanted their voice to be heard. "I tried to summarize the various points made by all of his supporters," wrote Jones in his book, *Behind the Dream*. "It was not easy; voices from every compass point were ringing in my head." According to Jones, King soon became frustrated, telling his advisors: "I am now going upstairs to my room to counsel with my Lord. I will see you tomorrow."

No doubt the magnitude of the task at hand weighed heavily on King's mind that night as he tried to rest. By this point, King was a well-known political figure, but few outside the Black church and activism circles had heard him speak publicly at length. With the relatively newfangled television networks preparing to project his

One of the many trains from New York arrives at Washington's Union Station for the march

DOWNTOWN CORE (LOWER EAST SIDE) NEW YORK

DOWNTOWN CORE

Clarence Jones, one of King's speech writers

The march was attended by a number of celebrities, including musicians Joan Baez and Bob Dylan

1876-1960

● **Jim Crow laws**
The enactment of racial segregation laws create 'separate but equal' status for African Americans, whose conditions were often inferior to those provided for White Americans.

1964

● **The Civil Rights Act**
One of the most sweeping pieces of equality legislation seen in the US, the Civil Rights Act prohibited discrimination of any kind and gave federal government the power to enforce desegregation.

1991

● **A stronger act**
President George HW Bush finally signs the Civil Rights Act of 1991, which strengthens existing civil rights law – but only after two years of debates and vetoes.

2009

● **The first Black president**
Barack Obama is sworn in as the 44th president of the United States – the first African American in history to become the US president.

WHAT YOU NEED TO KNOW ABOUT THE LANGUAGE OF THE SPEECH

Dr Catherine Brown, head of faculty and associate professor in English at New College of the Humanities, London

· "The speech derives its power from a combination of disparate elements. On one hand, it is addressed to a particular time and place, and emphasizes this fact: the situation is urgent; now is the time change must happen. On the other, the speech is dense with allusions to the Bible and foundational American documents and speeches.

· King is explicitly saying that the Emancipation Proclamation is a 'bad check' that has yet to be honored in regard to 'the Negro people', and the speech calls on that check to be honored.

· The other texts he refers to were not written by Black people, but by using their phrases and rhythms he is asserting his place – and the Black person's place – in the cultural, intellectual, and political tradition that they're part of. In his very words, he is not allowing himself to be 'separate but equal.'

· Behind the rhetoric of all these American texts is that of the King James translation of the Bible, and the rhetoric of ancient Greek and Roman orators. Both empires, and the authors of the Bible, are multi-ethnic; white supremacy would have been foreign to them."

image into the homes of millions, King knew that he must seize the unprecedented platform for civil rights.

When he was finally called to the podium, it was clear King's placement on the bill had put him at an immediate disadvantage. An oppressively hot day was quickly draining the crowd's enthusiasm and many had already left the march in order to make their long journeys home. A state-of-the-art sound system had been brought in for the day, but an act of sabotage before the event meant that even with help from the US Army Signal Corps in fixing it, some of the crowd struggled to hear the speakers. But King was a man who had endured death threats, bomb scares, multiple arrests, prison sentences, and constant intimidation in his pursuit for equality; he would not be undone by unfortunate circumstance.

Placing his typed yet scrawl-covered notes on the lectern, King began to speak, deftly

> "IN A HEARTBEAT, KING HAD DONE AWAY WITH HIS FORMAL ADDRESS AND BEGAN TO PREACH FROM HIS HEART HIS VISION"

and passionately, invoking the Declaration of Independence, the Emancipation Proclamation, and the US Constitution. Early on, he gave a nod toward Abraham Lincoln's Gettysburg Address ("Five score years ago. . . "), an equally iconic speech that, 100 years previously, set down the then-president's vision for human equality. King used rhythmic language, religious metaphor, and the repetition of a phrase at the beginning of each sentence: "One hundred years later. . . " he cries, highlighting Lincoln's failed dream. "We cannot be satisfied. . . " he says, declaring that "America has given the Negro people a bad check."

Jones, watching King captivate the crowd, breathed a sigh of relief. "A pleasant shock came over me as I realized that he seemed to be essentially reciting those suggested opening paragraphs I had scrawled down the night before in my hotel room," he reveals in *Behind the Dream*. Then something

Many of the leaders of the protest are held back before the March on Washington

IN THE PAPERS

Newspapers around the country brandished mixed headlines following King's speech. While many reported on the march's orderly and peaceful nature, several complained of the event's effects on traffic and transport in the area. Others, perhaps deliberately, gave the march only a few column inches, referring to it as a 'racial march' rather than a call for equality.

This front page from the Eugene Register Guard reflects the apprehension felt by many at the time. "Massive Negro Demonstration 'Only a Beginning'" is somewhat scare mongering, implying the US should be fearful of the Black population. The strapline "No Evidence of any Effect on Congress," meanwhile, seems to purposely undermine the efforts of those involved in the march.

unscripted happened. During a brief pause, gospel singer Mahalia Jackson, who had performed earlier in the day, shouted, "Tell 'em about the dream, Martin!" King pushed his notes to one side and stood tall in front of his audience. Jones, sensing what was about to happen, told the person next to him, "These people out there today don't know it yet, but they're about to go to church."

In a heartbeat, King had done away with his formal address and began to preach from

his heart his vision, his dream, which came to represent a legacy that would change civil rights forever. "I have a dream," he said, in one of the speech's most famous lines, "that my four little children will one day live in a nation where they will not be judged by the color of their skin but by the content of their character."

"Aw, sh**," remarked Walker Wyatt, another of King's advisors. "He's using the dream." Wyatt had previously advised King to stay away from his dream rhetoric. "It's trite, it's cliché. You've

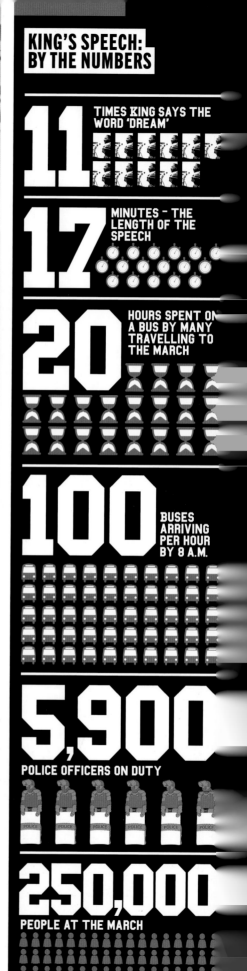

KING'S SPEECH: BY THE NUMBERS

11 TIMES KING SAYS THE WORD 'DREAM'

17 MINUTES – THE LENGTH OF THE SPEECH

20 HOURS SPENT ON A BUS BY MANY TRAVELLING TO THE MARCH

100 BUSES ARRIVING PER HOUR BY 8 A.M.

5,900 POLICE OFFICERS ON DUTY

250,000 PEOPLE AT THE MARCH

"I HAVE A DREA

Civil rights leaders of the March on Washington meet with John F. Kennedy in the Oval Office, August 28, 1963

used it too many times already," he warned. Indeed, King had used the refrain on several occasions before at fundraisers and rallies but, crucially, in the days before mass media it had not been publicised. To the millions watching on television and in person, the speech was as original as they come.

When King had talked about his 'dream' before, it had been generally well received, but certainly hadn't been groundbreaking. This time, however, it was different: thousands upon thousands of listening voices cried out in approval and unity, and King's final line: "Free at last, free at last, thank God Almighty – we are free at last!" was met with a rapturous standing ovation from the enormous crowd.

King's speech was a defining moment in African-American history and the fight for civil rights. "Though he was extremely well known before he stepped up to the lectern," Jones wrote, "he had stepped down on the other side of history." Even President Kennedy, no mean orator himself, reportedly turned to an aide and remarked: "He's damned good."

However, the clout of King's address was not entirely positive. The Federal Bureau of Investigation (FBI) was wary of King's activities, and its director J. Edgar Hoover considered King to be a dangerous radical. Two days after the march, FBI agent William C. Sullivan wrote a memo about King's increasing sway: "In the light of King's powerful demagogic speech yesterday he stands head and shoulders above all other Negro leaders put together when it comes to influencing great masses of Negroes. We must mark him now, if we have not done so before, as the most dangerous Negro [. . .] in this nation from the standpoint of communism, the Negro, and national security."

From this point on, King was targeted as a major enemy of the US and subjected to extensive surveillance and wiretapping by the FBI. According to Marshall Frady in his biography, *Martin Luther King Jr.: A Life*, the FBI even sent King intercepted recordings of his extramarital affairs in a thinly veiled attempt, King believed, to intimidate and drive him to suicide.

It seems incredible to believe, but contemporary criticism not only came from the

> **"KING WAS TARGETTED AS A MAJOR ENEMY OF THE US AND SUBJECTED TO EXTENSIVE SURVEILLANCE AND WIRETAPPING BY THE FBI"**

KENNEDY AND KING

King never publicly endorsed any political candidate, but he did reveal in 1960 that he "felt that Kennedy would make the best president."

Many claim Kennedy owed his presidency to King after securing his release from prison following a protest in Atlanta, Georgia – a gesture that helped gain a large proportion of the Black vote. But when the pair discussed the possibility of a second Emancipation Proclamation, Kennedy was slow to act.

Kennedy was caught between opposing forces: on one side, his belief in equality, and on the other, a preoccupation with foreign threats such as communism.

King delivers his iconic speech from the Lincoln Memorial

The March was attended by around 250,000 supporters

THE SPEECH'S LEGACY

Despite the success of King's speech, his address was largely forgotten afterwards, due to the speed of subsequent events, and to King's increasing disillusionment with his dream. He said that it had "turned into a nightmare." According to William P. Jones, author of The March on Washington, in the mid-1960s "most people would not have said it was the most powerful speech ever."

King's assassination led the nation to rediscover his speech, yet remarkably the full speech did not appear in writing until 15 years later, when a transcript was published in the Washington Post.

The original copy of the speech is currently owned by George Raveling. The then-26-year-old basketball player had volunteered at the last minute as a bodyguard during the march, and after King's speech asked him if he could have his notes. Raveling has been offered as much as $3 million for the original copy, but he says he has no intention of selling it.

establishment, but from King's peers. Civil rights activist and author Anne Moody made the trip to Washington, D.C., from Mississippi for the march and recalls: "I sat on the grass and listened to the speakers, to discover we had 'dreamers' instead of leaders leading us. Just about every one of them stood up there dreaming. Martin Luther King went on and on talking about his dream. I sat there thinking that in Canton we never had time to sleep, much less dream."

Human rights activist Malcolm X also famously condemned the march, as well as Dr. King's speech itself. Allegedly dubbing the event "the farce on Washington," he later wrote in his autobiography: "Who ever heard of angry revolutionaries swinging their bare feet together with their oppressor in lily pad pools, with gospels and guitars and 'I have a dream' speeches?"

Whatever some of the critics might have said, though, there was no doubt that King's speech singled him out as a leader. His oration has been lauded as one of the greatest of the 20th century, earned him the title of 'Man of the Year' by *Time Magazine*, and subsequently led to him receiving the Nobel Peace Prize. At the time, he was the youngest person to have been awarded the honor.

Most importantly, though, both the march and King's speech initiated debate and paved the way for genuine and tangible civil rights reforms, putting racial equality at the top of the agenda. The Civil Rights Act of 1964 – landmark legislation that outlawed discrimination based on race, color, religion, sex, or national origin – was enacted less than a year after King shared his dream.

Halfway through the speech, before doing away with his notes, Martin Luther King Jr. declared to his thousands of brothers and sisters in the crowd: "We cannot walk alone." That he spoke from his heart in such a poetic and unrepentant way ensured that, in the coming years, nobody did.

The casket of Martin Luther King Jr. was followed by more than 100,000 mourners

FOUR LITTLE GIRLS GONE

The terror bombing of the 16th Street Baptist Church in Birmingham killed four young girls and fuelled the ardor of the Civil Rights Movement

Four young girls were murdered with a bomb planted by white supremacist terrorists at the 16th Street Baptist Church

t was a heinous act of racially motivated hatred, and an entire nation, indeed the world, recoiled in horror. How could such violence, such terror happen in the United States of America?

However, in the segregated South of the 1960s, and particularly the city of Birmingham, Alabama, white supremacist terror bombings were all too common. The state's hub of industry and commerce also became its epicenter of racial unrest when leaders of the Civil Rights Movement chose the city as a focus for their efforts to end the era of Jim Crow and segregation.

While segregation was a way of life across the South, Alabama governor George Wallace and Birmingham commissioner of public safety 'Bull' Connor were staunch adversaries of the desegregation effort. Their public denunciation of equality among the races fomented turmoil. Connor was well known for employing brutal tactics to suppress demonstrators. Images of Birmingham police officers wielding clubs, fire hoses spraying on crowds, and vicious dogs straining against leashes were common fare on nightly network television news broadcasts.

Dr. Martin Luther King Jr., the acknowledged leader of the Civil Rights Movement and the nonviolent Southern Christian Leadership Conference, recognized that the increasing violence in Birmingham was the by-product of the city's racist reputation, not only due to the hostility of local government and its militantly active Ku Klux Klan (KKK) chapter, but also the fact that the desegregation effort was

centered there. Demonstrations and local meetings of civil rights activists often originated at the 16th Street Baptist Church, a predominantly Black congregation in the heart of the city. King himself had experienced the toxic local race relations in Birmingham in the spring of 1963, arrested there while leading nonviolent protests.

On August 28, 1963, King stood on the steps of the Lincoln Memorial in Washington, D.C., and delivered his stirring 'I Have a Dream' speech. Scarcely two weeks later, on September 15, about 200 members of the 16th Street Baptist Church were attending Sunday School and preparing for later services. At 10:22 a.m., a powerful explosion shattered the morning calm. Interior walls of the structure that had occupied the corner of 16th Street and 6th Avenue North since 1911 were demolished, shards of brick flew in every direction, stained glass windows 100 feet away were smashed, and an angry cloud billowed skyward. At least 15 sticks of dynamite had been planted on the east side of the church with a detonator set for Sunday morning, at a time when innocent people would surely be present.

Four young girls, 14-year-olds Carole Robertson, Addie Mae Collins, and Cynthia Wesley, and 11-year-old Denise McNair, were killed, their battered bodies recovered from a basement restroom. Twenty-two others were injured, including 12-year-old Sarah Collins, who lost an eye. Apparently in response to a federal court order to desegregate the public schools in the state of Alabama, the blast was

> **So many terror bombings occurred in Birmingham that the city was often called 'Bombingham'**

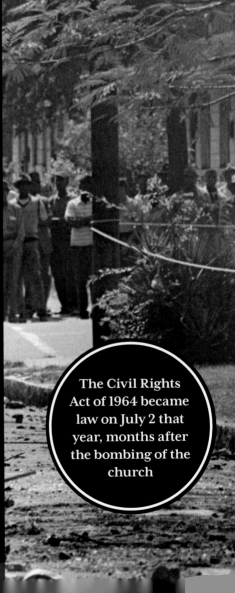

> **The Civil Rights Act of 1964 became law on July 2 that year, months after the bombing of the church**

JUSTICE DELAYED BUT DELIVERED

In the early 1970s, Alabama attorney general Bill Baxley reopened the case of the 16th Street Baptist Church bombing. The case had not grown cold due to lack of leads or evidence, but more correctly due to the indifference and outright stonewalling of the Federal Bureau of Investigation under the heavy hand of director J. Edgar Hoover, who led the FBI for decades and ordered the case closed in 1968 without action. Baxley charged Robert Edward Chambliss, also known as 'Dynamite Bob', who was convicted in 1977 and died in prison in 1985 while continuing to proclaim his innocence.

The second conviction did not occur for another 16 years. In 2001, Thomas Edwin Blanton Jr. was found guilty of murder. He remained in custody until his death in 2020. In 2002, Bobby Frank Cherry, a truck driver and welder, was also sentenced to life in prison. Considering himself a "political prisoner," he died behind bars in 2004. One of Cherry's sons, one of his four ex-wives, and an informant had testified against him at trial. A fourth probable conspirator, Herman Frank Cash, was never charged, although he was implicated as early as 1965. He died in 1994.

After his arrest for the 16th Street Baptist Church bombing in September 1963, Robert Edward Chambliss smiles for photographers

the third terror bombing in Birmingham in the span of 11 days.

In the wake of the tragedy, Dr. King addressed a gathering of 8,000 mourners at the funeral for three of the girls. He remarked, "These children – unoffending, innocent, and beautiful – were the victims of one of the most vicious and tragic crimes ever perpetrated against humanity." A wave of violence erupted across Birmingham. Two Black demonstrators were killed, and the National Guard was eventually deployed to restore order.

Although the perpetrators of the murders were probably well known, and specific individuals affiliated with the Birmingham KKK were identified, the wheels of justice turned slowly. The Federal Bureau of Investigation (FBI) gathered incriminating evidence against the suspects, but little was done under the administration of FBI director J. Edgar Hoover, an opponent of the Civil Rights Movement. After Hoover's death in 1972, the case was reopened on four separate occasions. Three of the four white supremacist suspects were convicted and sentenced to life in prison, the last of them brought to account 38 years after the incident. The fourth suspect died before he could be brought to trial.

The martyred children of the 16th Street Baptist Church did not die in vain. The bombing raised such an outcry against segregation that it surely hastened the reforms that followed in the turbulent decade of the 1960s.

> The Bible lesson at the church that fateful morning was from the Gospel of Matthew, advocating love and forgiveness

"AT LEAST 15 STICKS OF DYNAMITE HAD BEEN PLANTED ON THE EAST SIDE OF THE CHURCH, WITH A DETONATOR SET FOR SUNDAY MORNING"

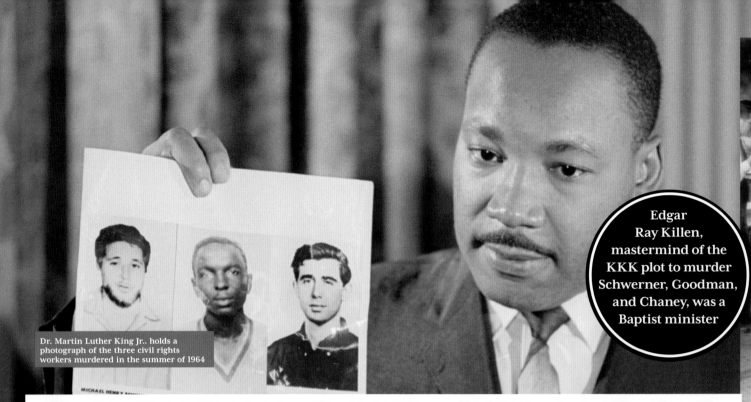

Dr. Martin Luther King Jr.. holds a photograph of the three civil rights workers murdered in the summer of 1964

Edgar Ray Killen, mastermind of the KKK plot to murder Schwerner, Goodman, and Chaney, was a Baptist minister

RACISM AND MURDER IN MISSISSIPPI

The murders of three civil rights workers in Mississippi gained national attention, though true justice may never have been served

Edgar Ray 'Preacher' Killen met his death just before his 93rd birthday sat behind bars at the state penitentiary in Parchman, convicted in the deaths of three civil rights workers in rural Mississippi in the summer of 1964. Killen's conviction as the mastermind of the murder conspiracy came in 2005, a full 41 years after the killings, not for murder but three counts of manslaughter, a lesser charge.

Justice, some say, has only been partially served to this day. The case is now closed after numerous reviews and charges against more than 20 individuals resulted in seven federal convictions for violations of the victims' human rights. The state of Mississippi would not initially indict the conspirators for murder, a state charge, and

with evidence collected by the Federal Bureau of Investigation (FBI), the verdicts were obtained in jury trials after the government in Washington invoked a 19th-century statute dating back to the era of post-Civil War reconstruction.

The summer of 1964 was pivotal in the progress of the Civil Rights Movement, particularly in the South. As the Council of Federated Organizations (COFO) and its affiliate, the Congress of Racial Equality (CORE), sent volunteers to Southern states, a concerted effort was underway to register Black voters. In Mississippi, white supremacists warned against a tidal wave of civil rights workers descending upon the state during their 'Freedom Summer' campaign.

Into this smoldering cauldron, 24-year-old Michael Schwerner, a civil rights worker from

New York, arrived in Meridian, Mississippi, in January 1964. On June 21, Schwerner returned from a training program in Ohio with 20-year-old Andrew Goodman, a new CORE volunteer from New York, and James Chaney, 21, a Black worker from Mississippi. Earlier in the month, two dozen Klansmen had descended on the Mount Zion Methodist Church in Neshoba County, beaten several people, and burned the building to the ground. They had been looking for Schwerner, who was planning to establish a 'Freedom School' at the church, the plan being to organize, educate, and mobilize African Americans.

On June 21, the three civil rights workers drove to the Zion Church site to investigate the terror attack. On their way back to Meridian, Neshoba County Sheriff's Deputy Cecil Price spotted their station wagon, a known

The charred station wagon driven by the civil rights workers murdered in Mississippi is discovered days after the crime

Demonstrators at the 1964 Democratic National Convention carry signs depicting the civil rights workers slain in Mississippi

> The 1988 film *Mississippi Burning* was loosely based on the events during the summer of 1964

The ranks of the Mississippi Ku Klux Klan, a vile hate group prone to violence, swelled to nearly 10,000 members by 1964, a year in which the shadowy white supremacist organization flexed its muscles with a campaign of intimidation and murder. Among the most common KKK tactics was the burning of a cross, a symbolic threat to those who were targeted, opposed the group, or promoted racial equality. On April 24, 1964, the Klan demonstrated its broad power base in Mississippi, holding simultaneous cross burnings at 61 locations across the state. During the violent summer that followed, the burnings of 20 predominantly Black churches were linked to the KKK.

For six weeks, FBI agents and others, including 400 US Navy personnel from a nearby naval air station, looked for the bodies of Michael Schwerner, Andrew Goodman, and James Chaney. In July, the search of the rivers, swamps, fields, and thickets yielded the bodies of eight Black men. One was recovered wearing a CORE T-shirt, and was obviously a victim of murder. Two others were identified as college students Charles Moore and Henry Dee, who had been abducted, severely beaten, and executed sometime in May. Another was identified as 14-year-old Herbert Oarsby. Little information about the other four corpses was ever disclosed.

The Klansmen themselves were warned that breaking their code of silence meant death, and compounding the difficulties encountered during the investigation was the simple fact that a number of the actual perpetrators and other members of the Klan held positions of authority in Neshoba County and throughout the area.

"IN FURTHER INSULT TO THE VICTIMS, NO ONE WAS EVER CHARGED WITH MURDER"

CORE vehicle, traveling near the town of Philadelphia. Price pulled the car over, arrested Chaney for speeding, and also handcuffed Goodman and Schwerner on a trumped up charge of possible collusion in the church burning. Late in the afternoon, the men were jailed in Philadelphia.

Requests to make phone calls were denied, and the three spent seven hours in jail supposedly waiting for a justice of the peace to handle the speeding fine. Around 10 p.m., Price allowed them to leave without coming before a court official. A member of the local KKK, Price had alerted other conspirators that the men were in custody. He followed them out of town and then returned to Philadelphia to drop off another police officer before again turning in pursuit. Price caught up with the men near the Neshoba County line and after two more vehicles arrived, Price loaded the three men in his patrol car. The three cars proceeded to a dirt lane called Rock Cut Road and stopped. Schwerner and Goodman were summarily shot in the heart. Chaney was beaten and then shot three times.

> At the height of the investigation into the murders, 200 FBI agents, many from New Orleans, were on the case

The CORE vehicle was set on fire along an abandoned logging road. It was found on June 23 during an exhaustive search for the missing men. The bodies were transported to a nearby farm and buried within a large earthen dam. After 44 days, FBI agents acting on a tip from an informant finally located them.

A series of indictments followed and in the 1967 trial, Price, Travis Barnette, Alton Roberts, Billy Wayne Posey, James Arledge, James Snowden, and Samuel Bowers were convicted of violating the slain trio's civil rights. Sentences ranged from three to ten years; however, none of them served longer than six years in prison. Eight defendants were acquitted, and three cases resulted in a hung jury. Killen remained free for decades. In further insult to the victims, no one was ever charged with murder.

Sometimes referred to as the 'Mississippi Burning' or 'Freedom Summer' murders, these needless and tragic deaths of three young men in June 1964 advanced the cause of civil rights, influencing the passage of the landmark Voting Rights Act of 1965.

Investigators uncover the remains of civil rights volunteers Schwerner, Goodman, and Chaney under thick red clay of an earthen dam

THE CIVIL RIGHTS ACT

The culmination of centuries of struggle and resistance, the Civil Rights Act of 1964 was a long overdue landmark, finally formalizing the equality promised by the Constitution

D espite growing calls for the enshrinement of Black rights, in line with the US Constitution, every single year between 1945 and 1957, Congress considered and failed to pass a bill guaranteeing universal civil rights. Although two Acts were passed in 1957 and 1960, they were stripped by fierce resistance of any teeth, becoming fairly inconsequential. However, they did result in the creation of the US Commission on Civil Rights, tasked with keeping the president informed on civil rights issues.

The move coincided with an upswell in support for the Civil Rights Movement, which culminated in the remarkable 250,000-person March on Washington for Jobs and Freedom, where Dr. Martin Luther King Jr. delivered his iconic 'I Have a Dream' speech, envisioning a time where Black and White people could live together as equals.

As pressure continued to build, President John F. Kennedy began to position the nation for a more sweeping Civil Rights Bill, meeting with Black representatives, while trying to build bipartisan support. Not even his untimely assassination could stop the momentum, as his successor, Lyndon B. Johnson, threw his support behind the campaign. Those in favor of the bill had to overcome the longest filibuster in American history, paralyzing the Senate for a gruelling 57 days, before it finally passed on July 2, 1964.

The Act not only strengthened the enforcement of voting rights and desegregation of schools, but outlawed discrimination on the basis of race, color, religion, sex, or national origin, while guaranteeing equal access to public places, employment, and schooling. However, some issue remained, leading Johnson to champion the Voting Rights Act, which banned literacy tests often used to disenfranchise Black voters, and appointed federal registrars to oversee elections. In the ensuing five years, the number of Black adults registered to vote almost doubled, reaching 65 percent.

Building on these gains, in 1968, just a week after the assassination of Martin Luther King Jr., Johnson signed the Fair Housing Act, outlawing discrimination in the rent, sale, or financing of housing. Decades later, while President Bush vetoed the Civil Rights Act of 1990, he later approved the 1991 Bill, which further reinforced the rights of employees to sue their employers for discrimination – enshrining right to trial by jury on discrimination claims.

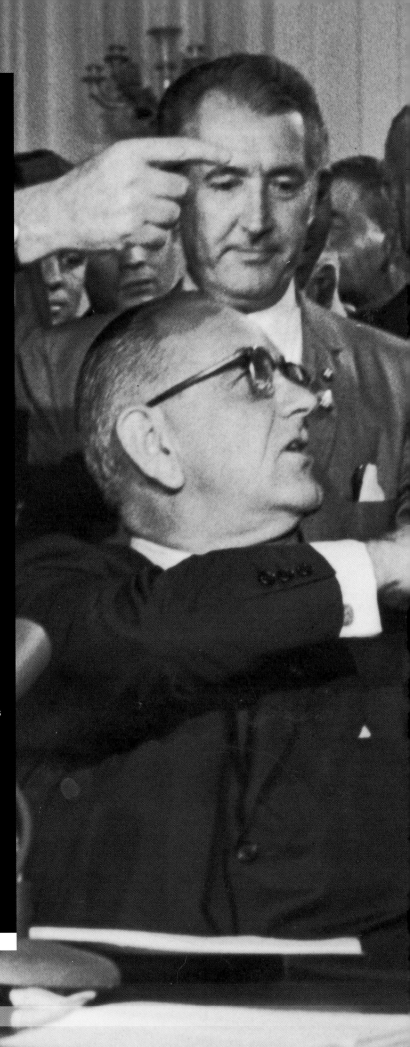

In 1964, decades of peaceful protest, courage, and adversity culminated in the long-overdue Civil Rights Bill

Previous efforts to legislate civil rights were nullified by the efforts of opponents, such as Senator Strom Thurmond, who set a record filibuster of 24 hours 18 minutes in 1957

Martin Luther King shakes hands with President Johnson at the signing of the Civil Rights Act

THE LONG MARCH TO VOTE

While the Civil Rights Act had outlawed discrimination, in the South many African Americans were still effectively disenfranchised. In 1964, the struggle turned to the right to vote

Participants in the Selma to Montgomery marches in 1965

On the last day, marchers move along Dexter Avenue to the State Capitol building

Civil rights marchers in front of the State Capitol building at the end of their march from Selma to Montgomery

On July 2, 1964, President Lyndon Johnson had signed the Civil Rights Act, outlawing discrimination on the basis of color, race, religion, or sex. But while the passage of the act through Congress and the Senate was a historic achievement, Black people in Southern states still faced entrenched discrimination, in particular with respect to voting rights. For instance, the Alabama state legislature required people registering to vote to pass a literacy test and pay a poll tax. What made the discrimination even more invidious was the test being administered by White people whose judgement was final and often arbitrary. Every effort was made to make it difficult for Black people to even attempt to register, with restricted opening hours for centers of registration (often only one or two days a month), intimidation, and threats of sacking to anyone who did try to register to vote. The end result was that in Dallas County, Alabama, according to a 1961 report, only 130 Black people were registered to vote, out of a population of 15,000 eligible voters. Dallas County, with Selma as its county seat, had a majority of Black citizens but, because so many were disenfranchised, political power there lay in the hands of the White minority – and they intended to keep it.

Local activists in Selma and Dallas County had made repeated attempts to register voters but when these failed, eight people invited the Southern Christian Leadership Conference (SCLC) to assist in gaining local Black people their rights. One of the factors that led the SCLC board, including Dr. Martin Luther King Jr., to accept the invitation was the reputation the Dallas County police force, under its sheriff, Jim Clark, had for brutality. Clark employed 200 deputies, some of whom were members of the Ku Klux Klan, arming them with electric cattle prods. Dr. King and the SCLC had learned that time-honored rule of the news media: if it bleeds, it leads. To garner the national attention they needed in order to put pressure on President Lyndon Johnson to bring forward legislation against the sort of discrimination Black voters faced in places like Selma, they needed to find city authorities that were brutal enough and stupid enough to attack and beat nonviolent protestors under the lenses of TV cameramen. In Sheriff Jim Clark, King and the SCLC had found their man.

As the first stage in the campaign, Dr. King, the SCLC, and local activists organized mass voter registrations to highlight the invidious restrictions placed on Black voters. Unable to suppress their violent bigotry, Sheriff Clark and his men responded brutally and over 3,000 people were arrested through January 1965, including Dr. King. But despite a court ruling in favor of the civil rights protestors, by February Dr. King could still say, in a letter to the *New York Times*, "This is Selma, Alabama. There are more Negroes in jail with me than there are on the voting rolls."

Then, on February 18, 1965, police broke up a protest in neighboring Perry County. Trying to escape the Alabama state police, Jimmie Lee Jackson, a poor farm worker who was also a deacon in his church, took refuge in a café but the police followed him in and then shot him. Jackson managed to stagger out, but died eight days later from his wounds.

Jackson's death stoked emotions that were already running high. In order to stop the

Civil rights marchers cross the Edmund
Pettus Bridge in Selma, Alabama

Marchers were greeted with violence. This image shows civil rights leader John Lewis being beaten by police

"We March with Selma!": Protestors in New York carry banners in support of the Selma to Montgomery marchers

protests turning violent, SCLC organizer James Bevel proposed a march from Selma, the county seat, to Montgomery, the state capital, a distance of 50 miles, to present their grievances to the governor. Dr. King was in Atlanta, so the march was led by the Reverend Hosea Williams along with student activist, John Lewis.

On Sunday 7 March, about 600 marchers set out from Selma and came to the Edmund Pettus Bridge over the Alabama River. The bridge has a central hump, so it was only when they crested the hump that the marchers realized that the police and state troopers were waiting for them on the other side. The governor of Alabama, George Wallace, had ordered that the march was to be prevented from reaching Montgomery by any means necessary: Sheriff Jim Clark needed no further encouragement. With his mounted posse, Clark charged into the marchers, beating them with clubs while police fired tear gas. Even when the protestors tried to retreat, the mounted police charged after them, still flailing with their clubs.

That evening, ABC, one of the national networks, stopped its programming to show viewers film of the brutality visited, by American lawmen, upon nonviolent protestors. The following day, the national press was

covered with pictures of police beating women and men. Sheriff Jim Clark, too stupid to stop himself or his men, had fallen for the trap that had been set for him.

In response to the violence, Dr. King called on local religious leaders to join him in a second march from Selma to Montgomery that would take place two days later, on Tuesday March 9. But when Judge Frank Minis Johnson placed a temporary restraining order on the march, Dr. King and the other protest leaders were faced with a dilemma. Judge Johnson had given many rulings in favor of Black civil rights and it was thought that he would lift the order. In the end, Dr. King led some 2,000 marchers to Edmund Pettus Bridge where they knelt and prayed, in sight of Alabama state troopers, before turning around and returning to Selma. As a result, the day became known as 'Turnaround Tuesday'. But the protestors' nonviolence was again met by violence – that evening James Reeb, a White Unitarian Universalist minister who had joined in the march, was set on by segregationists and beaten badly. He died two days later from his injuries.

On March 15, President Lyndon Johnson addressed a joint session of Congress, and the whole nation via television, saying, "Their cause must be our cause too. Because it is not just Negroes, but really it is all of us, who must overcome the crippling legacy of bigotry and injustice. And we shall overcome." Two days later, the president brought new legislation to ensure voting rights for Black people before Congress. Meanwhile, Judge Johnson had lifted the restraining order against the marchers while also directing local law enforcement that they were not to harass the marchers.

On March 21, the third march to Montgomery left Selma, protected by FBI agents. Among the marchers were Joe Young, a blind man from Georgia, and Jim Letherer from Michigan, who did the march on crutches. The marchers took four days to reach the state capital and the weather was often foul, but by the time they reached Montgomery the number of marchers had grown to 25,000. On their last night, as the marchers camped in the grounds of St. Jude, a Catholic

Defining moment

Freedom Day Oct 7, 1963
Around 400 Black people arrive at Dallas County Courthouse to register to vote. Annie Lee Cooper is one of the people waiting in line. The registrars work as slowly as possible and take a very long lunch break. But Freedom Day marks the beginning of the struggle for the vote in Dallas County, and Alabama more generally.

● **Dr. King arrested**
Leading a protest, Dr. Martin Luther King is arrested and put into Selma jail. **February 1, 1965**

● **Political progress**
President Lyndon Johnson says he will urge legislation for voting rights to be considered by Congress. **February 6, 1965**

Timeline

963 1965

● **Start of the campaign**
Dr. King begins the campaign. Some 700 Black people come to a meeting at Brown Chapel despite a court injunction forbidding such gatherings. **January 2, 1965**

● **First attempts to register**
Dr. King leads 300 marchers to the courthouse to attempt to register for the vote. Nobody manages to register. **January 18, 1965**

● **Further attempts to register**
This time, when people come to try to register, Sheriff Clark arrests them. **January 19, 1965**

● **Punching back**
Annie Lee Cooper, waiting to register, slugs Sheriff Clark when he pokes her with his club. She is arrested. **January 25, 1965**

● **Death in the café**
Jimmie Lee Jackson, hiding from state troopers in a café, is shot in the stomach. He dies eight days later. **February 18, 1965**

Children lead the marchers into Montgomery towards the State Capitol building on the last day of the third march

Demonstrators lock arms in front of the Dallas County courthouse in Selma, Alabama. Sheriff Jim Clark had them all arrested

establishment on the outskirts of Montgomery, entertainers such as Harry Belafonte and Nina Simone performed for the excited crowd. On the morrow, they knew they would be making history.

On March 25, Dr. King led the marchers through Montgomery. In response to reports of snipers waiting to shoot him, 15 Black clergymen who looked like King walked abreast of him at the front of the procession. However, when the marchers reached the State Capitol building, Governor Wallace refused to see them. Dr. King proceeded to address the marchers and, via television, the nation.

"Our aim must never be to defeat or humiliate the White man, but to win his friendship and understanding. We must come to see that the end we seek is a society at peace with itself, a society that can live with its conscience. And that will be a day not of the White man, not of the Black man. That will be the day of man as man."

Less than six months later, on August 6, 1965, President Johnson signed the Voting Rights Act, with Dr. King and other civil rights leaders by his side.

THE WOMAN WHO DID NOT TURN THE OTHER CHEEK

Based as it was in Christianity, the Civil Rights Movement enjoined its activists to practice nonviolence, to turn the other cheek as Jesus had told his disciples, and the movement's followers kept to this precept with astonishing self-discipline and courage. However, under the sorts of provocation people faced, tempers could snap, and no one's temper snapped more famously than that of Annie Lee Cooper. A Selma native, she had moved when young to Kentucky, before returning to Selma in 1962 to look after her mother. Cooper

Cooper was played by Oprah Winfrey in the movie Selma

had registered to vote when she lived in Kentucky and Ohio, and she was determined to vote in Alabama too, but first she had to register. She tried often, to no avail. "Once," she said, "I stood in line from 7 a.m. to 4 p.m. but never got to register." On October 7, 1963, activists organized a Freedom Day when 400 Black people, the maximum allowed by the courts, waited outside Dallas County courthouse to register, and Annie Lee Cooper stood among them. She wasn't able to register, but when her employers saw her there, they fired her. On January 25, 1965, Annie Lee Cooper tried again, joining the queue of Black people waiting outside Dallas County courthouse to register to vote. But this time, Sheriff Jim Clark turned up with his deputies. Clark ordered Cooper to leave, prodding her in the neck with his club, until Annie Lee Cooper finally let go of the principles of nonviolence, swung around, and landed a sweet right hook on Clark's jaw, knocking him to the ground. Clark's deputies then waded in, pushing Cooper down and holding her there while the enraged Jim Clark beat her with his club. Annie Lee Cooper was arrested and held for 11 hours in jail: she sang spirituals during her imprisonment.

Defining moment
Bloody Sunday **March 7, 1965**
Not knowing what's waiting for them on the other side of Edmund Pettus Bridge, 600 marchers cross the Alabama River only to come face-to-face with Sheriff Jim Clark (left) and his deputies, mounted on horses, ready, and spoiling for a fight. The police and state troopers attack the marchers, putting 16 in the hospital and injuring at least 50 others. Pictures dominate the TV channels and newspapers.

Defining moment
March to Montgomery
March 25, 1965
The third march from Selma to Montgomery finally reaches the intended destination and does so without injury or violence. Outside the State Capitol, Dr. Martin Luther King Jr. asks, rhetorically, how long Black people will have to wait for their right to vote. The answer: "Not long, because the arc of the moral universe is long, but it bends toward justice."

Court orders
The day after Bloody Sunday, Judge Frank Johnson, concerned for their safety, places a temporary injunction against further marches.
March 8, 1965

Turnaround Tuesday
Dr. King leads marchers to Edmund Pettus Bridge, prays there, then leads them back to Selma.
March 9, 1965

Death of the minister
James Reeb, with three other ministers, is attacked by the Ku Klux Klan. Reeb dies from his injuries two days later. He was 38.
March 11, 1965

On the road again
Marchers set out for the third time from Selma, heading to Montgomery, the state capital.
March 21, 1965

Death in the night
Viola Liuzzo, a White Unitarian Universalist minister and mother of five who had come to Montgomery to help with the march, was shot by the Ku Klux Klan in her car.
March 25, 1965

MALCOLM

MARTIN

Inside the rivalry that supercharged the Civil Rights Movement

EXPERT BIO

Dr. Peniel E. Joseph is an American scholar, teacher, and public speaker with a focus on race issues. He holds a joint professorship at the LBJ School of Public Affairs and the History Department in the College of Liberal Arts at The University of Texas at Austin. His book, *The Sword And The Shield: The Revolutionary Lives Of Malcolm X And Martin Luther King Jr.*, was released in March 2020

All illustrations by Kevin McGivern

© Getty Images

They didn't hold high public office, they didn't fight wars, and they didn't possess vast wealth and riches, and yet Dr. Martin Luther King Jr. and Malcolm X still managed to become two of the most iconic figures of the 20th century. Rising to prominence at the height of the Civil Rights Movement in the 1960s, each became equally revered and reviled by different parts of the United States. Both would ultimately come to be the de facto leader of their groups and each would meet an untimely and violent end at the hands of assailants whose identities and motives continue to be hotly debated.

In Dr. King's role as first president of the Southern Christian Leadership Conference and Malcolm X's position as a minister and leading national spokesperson for the Nation of Islam (NOI), these two men often appeared to offer two conflicting arguments and approaches to the challenge of achieving racial justice and equality in America. What's more, each existed in the public eye to a far greater and wider extent than any of their contemporaries

RIGHT
It was Malcolm X who introduced Muhammad Ali to the Nation of Islam

MIDDLE-RIGHT
King attends the Ghana independence ceremony in 1957

BOTTOM-RIGHT
Speaking at a rally in Harlem in 1963, Malcolm X points to a photo of a dead Black protestor

BELOW
A mugshot for Malcolm Little, aged 18 when he was arrested in 1944

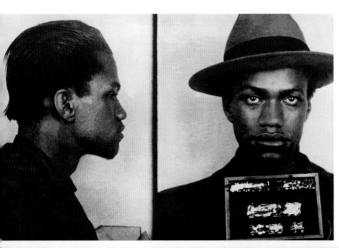

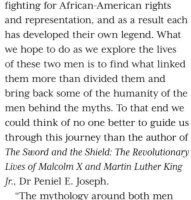

fighting for African-American rights and representation, and as a result each has developed their own legend. What we hope to do as we explore the lives of these two men is to find what linked them more than divided them and bring back some of the humanity of the men behind the myths. To that end we could think of no one better to guide us through this journey than the author of *The Sword and the Shield: The Revolutionary Lives of Malcolm X and Martin Luther King Jr.*, Dr Peniel E. Joseph.

"The mythology around both men frames them as opposites," he explains. "It frames Malcolm as Dr. King's evil twin. It frames Dr. King as this saint who would just give everybody a hug if he was alive right now and that really takes away from understanding the depth and breadth of their political power, their political radicalism, and their evolution over time."

We'll take a closer look at that evolution and convergence of ideas as we progress, but first it's interesting to consider where each man came from and how that might have informed his world view. "Martin Luther King Jr. is raised in an upper-middle class, elite household in Atlanta, Georgia," Joseph tells us. "His father is a preacher, his mother is present in his life, and it's a very comfortable upbringing. Malcolm X is raised in Omaha and in Lansing, Michigan on farms, so he's a country boy. His father is murdered by white supremacists when he's six years old and his mother is put in a psychiatric facility, so he's a foster child by the time he's in elementary school. And then he becomes a hustler in Boston and Harlem as a teenager and he's finally arrested for theft and spends seven years in prison. When Malcolm is in prison, Dr. King is at Morehouse College, the most

CIVIL RIGHTS TIMELINE — Important milestones towards justice

May 17, 1954
BROWN V BOARD OF EDUCATION
The United States Supreme Court makes the landmark ruling that segregation of students on the basis of race is unconstitutional, essentially ending all-White school policies and the 'separate but equal' rules of Jim Crow.

December 1, 1955
ROSA PARKS
As part of an ongoing and organized protest against the segregation of buses in Alabama, Rosa Parks refuses to give up her seat when the driver moves the dividing line of the bus back, sparking a bus boycott in Montgomery, Alabama, and focusing national attention on the issue.

September 1957
THE LITTLE ROCK NINE
Nine African American students attend Little Rock Central High School for the first time; a school that had been all-White up until that point. A large mob and members of the Arkansas National Guard block their path to the school, ultimately requiring the students to have military protection to enter after weeks of protest.

February 1, 1960
THE GREENSBORO FOUR
Four students begin a sit-in at the whites-only lunch counter of Woolworth department store. Denied service, they refuse to leave when asked and remain seated until closing. They return again the next day with 20 more students, with the sit-in growing in the following weeks to take up every seat.

November 14, 1960
RUBY BRIDGES
Six-year-old Ruby Bridges hopes to attend the previously all-White school of William Frantz Elementary in New Orleans. She requires an armed escort by federal marshals to navigate the angry mob leading up to and outside the school. This continues every day of the school year and she is taught alone in an empty classroom by her teacher, Barbara Henry.

prestigious, historically Black, all-men's college that you could go to then or now. He goes and gets a theological degree at seminary school – Crozer Theological Seminary in Chester, Pennsylvania – and then gets a PhD at Boston University."

The strong religious upbringing of King clearly had a massive influence on his life, becoming a preacher himself as well as a political activist and integrating his faith deep into his speeches. Meanwhile, Malcolm's tough upbringing and the tragedies he endured help to explain the righteous anger and pain he expressed as a minister for the NOI. However, Joseph does point out one curious similarity in their upbringing: "They're both impacted by the movie Gone With the Wind. It premieres in Atlanta when Dr. King is ten years old. Malcolm is 14 years old and sees that movie in Mason, Michigan, and talks about squirming in the movie theater at all the racial stereotypes that the movie's filled with. It's filled with Black women who are servants who are getting slapped in the face by White women who are masters, and it's this sepia-toned, nostalgic vision of racial slavery. So that's similar."

It was during his time in prison for burglary that the then-Malcolm Little was introduced to Islam by some of his siblings and he joined the NOI. Its leader Elijah Muhammad took a personal interest in him, with letters being sent between them, before he was released in 1952. He abandoned his 'slave name' of Little and became Malcolm X, a minister in the NOI advocating for Black separatism (which was the policy of the organization), first in Chicago and

"THE MYTHOLOGY AROUND BOTH MEN FRAMES THEM AS OPPOSITES"

later in Harlem, New York, which would become his base for years to come. The formative years of each man's life are ultimately what frames them as polarized voices in a similar struggle.

"Malcolm X is really Black America's prosecuting attorney and he is going to be charging White America with a series of crimes against Black humanity," explains Joseph. "I argue in *The Sword and the Shield* that in a way his life's work boils down to radical Black dignity, and what he means by Black dignity is really Black people having the political self-determination to decide their own political futures and fates. They define racism and they define anti-racism and what social justice looks like for themselves. It's connected to the United States, but globally it's also connected to African decolonization, African independence, Third World independence, Middle East politics, all of it." Radical Black dignity is also, importantly, about building up a Black cultural identity that is independent of White America and building self-worth, which is a big part of where ideas like Black Power would later come from.

King naturally comes to things from a different direction. "Martin Luther King Jr. is really the defense attorney," says Joseph. "He defends Black lives to White people and White lives to Black people. He's really advocating for radical Black citizenship and his notion of citizenship is going to get more expansive over time; it's going to be more than just voting rights and ending segregation. It's going to become about ending poverty, food justice, health care, a living wage,

---

May 4, 1961
THE FREEDOM RIDES
Following the protests of the bus boycott started by Rosa Parks, the Freedom Rides are intended to test new rulings banning segregation on interstate travel. Seven African American and six White protesters board two buses and face violence in South Carolina on May 14 when a bus is forced to stop to change a tire.

April 3, 1963
BIRMINGHAM
The Birmingham, Alabama, demonstrations against segregation encompass sit-ins, boycotts, mass protests, and marches to City Hall. Martin Luther King Jr. is arrested on April 12 for violating anti-protest rules. The authorities use fire hoses and dogs against protesters, causing national outrage and prompting JFK to propose a Civil Rights Bill.

August 28, 1963
MARCH ON WASHINGTON
The March on Washington for Jobs and Freedom is the culmination of protests throughout 1963. An estimated 250,000 people gather peacefully on the National Mall in Washington, D.C., where they hear speeches from Civil Rights leaders like a young John Lewis and, famously, Martin Luther King's 'I Have a Dream' speech.

July 2, 1964
CIVIL RIGHTS ACT
Picking up and strengthening the proposal by President Kennedy before his assassination, Lyndon B. Johnson signs the Civil Rights Act into law. It is intended to end racial discrimination in the workplace and in finding employment, end voter discrimination, and end segregation of public facilities.

March 7, 1965
THE SELMA MARCH
A march from Selma in Alabama to Montgomery is organized to protest against voting discrimination and to advocate for a federal voting law. The attempt is met with vicious violence by state troopers. A second attempt led by King is stopped short when troopers appear to make way for them. A final attempt on March 21 is completed, with 25,000 in attendance.

> "True peace is not merely the absence of tension; it is the presence of justice"
>
> *September 17, 1958*

> "Injustice anywhere is a threat to justice everywhere"
>
> *April 16, 1963*

> "This is no time to engage in the luxury of cooling off or to take the tranquilizing drug of gradualism"
>
> *April 16, 1963*

> "True compassion is more than flinging a coin to a beggar. It comes to see that an edifice which produces beggars needs restructuring"
>
> *April 4, 1967*

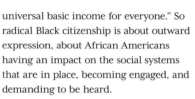

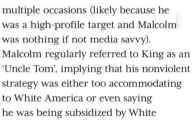

ABOVE
Police use fire hoses to subdue protesters in Birmingham, Alabama, in 1963

RIGHT
Malcolm X gives a speech in Harlem, which became his political home base

MIDDLE-RIGHT
King met President Johnson on a number of occasions, but the meetings declined as King pushed for more radical reforms

BOTTOM-RIGHT
Malcolm X meets Prince Faisal al-Saud, who would later become king of Saudi Arabia

universal basic income for everyone." So radical Black citizenship is about outward expression, about African Americans having an impact on the social systems that are in place, becoming engaged, and demanding to be heard.

These two approaches, one that builds personal identity and another that looks to express that identity and have it recognized by a system that's set up to ignore Black voices, seem more complementary than adversarial when we look at them from a slight remove. "Their differences really become differences of tactics rather than goals," says Joseph. "They're both going to come to see that you need dignity and citizenship and those goals are going to converge over time, but it's the tactics and how we get to those goals."

Famously, though, they did not always see eye to eye. Malcolm X in particular took aim at King and the Southern Christian Leadership Conference on multiple occasions (likely because he was a high-profile target and Malcolm was nothing if not media savvy). Malcolm regularly referred to King as an 'Uncle Tom', implying that his nonviolent strategy was either too accommodating to White America or even saying he was being subsidized by White America to keep African Americans defenseless. King for his part warned, "Fiery, demagogic oratory in the Black ghettos, urging Negroes to arm themselves and prepare to engage in violence, as [Malcolm X] has done, can reap nothing but grief."

And yet despite the animosity between the two men publicly, Malcolm X continually attempted to reach out to King over the years. He sent articles and NOI reading materials and invited him to speeches and meetings. On July 31, 1963, Malcolm X even publicly called for unity. "If capitalistic Kennedy and communistic Khrushchev can find

"THEIR DIFFERENCES REALLY BECOME DIFFERENCES OF TACTICS RATHER THAN GOALS"

"We are nonviolent with people who are nonviolent with us"
1963

"We didn't land on Plymouth Rock, Plymouth Rock landed on us"
March 29, 1964

"We can never get civil rights in America until our human rights are first restored"
August 25, 1964

"You can't separate peace from freedom because no one can be at peace unless he has his freedom"
April 4, 1967

Image source: wikif/Lyndon Baines Johnson Library and Museum

something in common on which to form a United Front despite their tremendous ideological differences, it is a disgrace for Negro leaders not to be able to submerge our 'minor' differences in order to seek a common solution to a common problem posed by a Common Enemy," he wrote, inviting civil rights leaders to join him in Harlem to speak at a rally. But they did not attend, perhaps because shortly after they would be attending the March on Washington and they were deep in planning. The slight was taken, though, with Malcolm dismissing the August 1963 event the 'Farce on Washington'.

Despite the rhetoric, Joseph thinks Malcolm was still learning much from King's activities. "Dr. King is the person who helps mobilize Birmingham, Alabama, in 1963 and King is going to be facing German Shepherds and fire hoses and it's going to be a big, global media spectacle," he says. "King writes his famous 'Letter from Birmingham Jail' during that period. Malcolm is in Washington, D.C., for most of that spring as temporary head of Mosque No. 4 there and he's really going to be influenced by King's mobilizations – his ability to mobilize large numbers of people – even as he's critical of King because of the nonviolence and the fact

that so many kids and women are being brutalized."

The really big shift in world view for Malcolm X comes the following year as he gradually breaks away from Elijah Muhammad (who was mired in allegations of extramarital affairs) and the NOI and seeks to define his own path forward. "By 1964 in 'The Ballot or the Bullet' speech, you see Malcolm X talking about voting rights as part of Black liberation and freedom. You see him in an interview with Robert Penn Warren saying that he and Dr. King have the same goal, which is human dignity, but they have different ways of getting there," explains Joseph.

It's around this time that Malcolm X left the United States for several months, traveling to Egypt, Lebanon, Liberia, Senegal, Nigeria, Ghana, and Saudi Arabia, including taking his pilgrimage to Mecca where he received his new Islamic name, El-Hajj Malik El-Shabazz. The trip made a big impression on him, and he spoke subsequently about how seeing Muslims of so many different ethnic and cultural backgrounds worshipping together opened his eyes to the real possibility of racial integration and peace.

All of this actually took place not long after the two men had met for what would be the first and only time. In the midst of the passing of the Civil Rights Act, as it was being filibustered on the Senate floor, Dr. Martin Luther King Jr.

and Malcolm X crossed paths on Capitol Hill. "They both come and are talking to reporters and doing press conferences in support of the Civil Rights Act," says Joseph. "They're both coming there for the same reason. People are surprised that Malcolm is there and he's watching the Senate and he's doing his interviews and there's a point where Malcolm is in the same room as Dr. King and on the couch while Dr. King is doing his press conference and they meet afterwards, exchanging pleasantries." It was a moment captured by only a couple of photos, catching them mid-conversation with Malcolm recorded as saying, "I'm throwing myself into the heart of the civil rights struggle."

Malcolm X continued to make overtures to King in the months that followed, offering him protection in St. Augustine, Florida, that spring as protestors fought for desegregation of its beaches and playgrounds and later in Selma, Alabama, as King's attention turned to voting rights where he felt he had a role to play. "I think Malcolm gave King more room to operate and I think Malcolm knew this," says Joseph. "When he visits Selma shortly before his own death, he's trying to visit Dr. King in February of 1965 in Alabama but King is jailed and he gets to visit Coretta Scott King, gives a speech and visits some of the student organizers. He tells Coretta Scott King that he's only there to support her husband and

"KING BECOMES THIS VERY PROPHETIC, RADICAL FIGURE AFTER MALCOLM'S ASSASSINATION"

ABOVE
The only time the two men met was on Capitol Hill in 1964

he wants people to know that if her husband's advocacy of voting rights is not accomplished that there are other alternative forces out there that are going to be led by him. So he definitely offers King more strategic leeway."

Whether or not the two men could have ultimately found a way to coordinate their approaches in a less ad hoc fashion we will never know because on February 21, 1965, just days before the Selma to Montgomery marches were about to be attempted by King's movement, Malcolm X was assassinated in New York. The exact details remain disputed, but we do know that he was about to speak at the Audubon Ballroom, where he was expected to announce plans for voter registration drives, denounce police brutality, and call for the UN to speak up on human rights violations in America. As he began to speak a scuffle broke out, likely as a distraction, and a man approached the stage with a shotgun, shooting him. Two more men rushed the stage with pistols and shot him again as he lay on the floor. The impact of his death would be felt throughout the movement, and quite profoundly by King.

"One of the surprising things is that we don't discuss the way in which the person who is most radicalized by Malcolm's assassination is Martin Luther King Jr.," Joseph explains. "He breaks with Lyndon Johnson on April 4, 1967 with the Riverside Church speech in New York, where he says that the United States is the greatest purveyor of violence in the world. Malcolm

BELOW
The events of Bloody Sunday in Selma, Alabama, shocked the world

TOP
King gives his 'I Have a Dream' speech on the National Mall

ABOVE & RIGHT
Malcolm X was critical of the March on Washington, but it mobilized hundreds of thousands of people

The people who helped shape the Civil Rights Movement of the 1960s

MARCUS GARVEY

AUG 17, 1887 - JUNE 10, 1940

An early proponent of Black Nationalism, Marcus Garvey believed in a pan-African movement that involved global mobilization of Black people against oppression. He founded the Universal Negro Improvement Association and even launched the Black Star Line to build trade links between Africa and America.

BAYARD RUSTIN

MARCH 17, 1912 - AUG 24, 1987

One of Martin Luther King Jr.'s closest advisors and one of the organizers of the March on Washington in 1963, Rustin grew up in a Quaker family who were heavily involved in the NAACP. As well as fighting for civil rights, Rustin was also openly gay and faced further discrimination both within and outside the movement.

ELIJAH MUHAMMAD

OCT 7, 1897 - FEB 25, 1975

The man who would become the head of the Nation of Islam was born to former-slave sharecroppers in Georgia. He took over the NOI from its founder Wallace D. Fard after he mysteriously disappeared. He was a strong advocate for Black separatism and helped develop Malcolm X and his own successor, Louis Farrakhan.

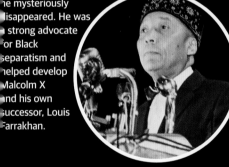

FANNIE LOU HAMER

OCT 6, 1917 - MARCH 14, 1977

Joining the movement in 1962 to fight for voting rights, Hamer was fired from her job because of her activism. In 1964 she co-founded the Mississippi Freedom Democratic Party, which challenged for speaking time at the Democratic Convention. Her testimony before the DNC Credentials Committee garnered national attention.

ELLA BAKER

DEC 13, 1903 - DEC 13, 1986

While Baker worked with Martin Luther King Jr. as director of the SCLC, her commitment to mobilizing Black youth in America saw her split from King in 1960 to form the independent Student Nonviolent Coordinating Committee, focused on grassroots organizing over the top-down leadership she saw elsewhere.

STOKELY CARMICHAEL

JUNE 29, 1941 - NOV 15, 1998

The originator of the rallying cry of 'Black Power', Stokely Carmichael (later known as Kwame Ture) originally joined the SNCC (and became its chairman) before seeking a more militant path closer to that of Malcolm X. He ultimately aligned more with the newly formed Black Panther Party and moved to Guinea.

and how racial slavery had shaped the present and King talks about that much more after 1965. He's in Marks, Mississippi, helping to lead the Poor People's Campaign and he's in tears because there's so much poverty there. He says that what the people in Marks, Mississippi, are experiencing is a crime and they're going to go to Washington, D.C. Malcolm had always said that Black poverty, racial segregation, and violence were crimes, but Martin Luther King starts speaking in that language."

As King turns his attention to economic inequality through the mid to late-1960s, he digs deeper and deeper into the wider historic inequalities and injustices of America. "He becomes this very prophetic, radical figure after Malcolm's assassination and he's much more interested in race and blackness too," says Joseph. "There's a speech he makes in 1967 where he says they even tell you 'A white lie is better than a black lie'. He gets into it in a granular way; and this is King, not Malcolm. It's Dr. King who says that the halls of the US Congress are 'running wild with racism'. King is testifying before the Kerner Commission, the president's riot commission, and talking about the depth and breadth of White racism. He speaks to the American Psychological Association in September 1967 and says that White people in the United States are producing chaos, blame Black people for the chaos, and say there would be peace if not for the chaos that they produce. He's really much more candid and much more blunt, much more radical, much more revolutionary and there are no more meetings with the president of the United States."

It is perhaps because they evolved and were willing to learn from one another that each has remained as relevant today as they were in the 1960s. "Even in 2020 with George Floyd and Black Lives Matter and these global protest movements, the only way to understand these movements is to understand Malcolm and Martin who were talking about so much of these issues of police brutality and the criminal justice system, racial segregation, and poverty and state-sanctioned violence," says Joseph.

Which is why, adds Joseph, that getting beyond the mythology of these men is so important. "What did they actually do? What did they think? What were the networks that they connected with? Because both of them are in these really important networks with people like

The Sword and the Shield: The Revolutionary Lives of Malcolm X And Martin Luther King Jr. by Dr Peniel E. Joseph is available now from Basic Books

THE SWORD AND THE SHIELD

THE REVOLUTIONARY LIVES OF MALCOLM X AND MARTIN LUTHER KING JR

PENIEL E. JOSEPH

RIGHT
Today both Malcolm and Martin are frequently depicted together by activists

BELOW
President Lyndon B. Johnson signs the Civil Rights Act with King in attendance

BOTTOM
Malcolm was unable to finish the work of creating a more international movement for racial justice

"IT'S DR. KING WHO SAYS THAT THE HALLS OF THE US CONGRESS ARE 'RUNNING WILD WITH RACISM'"

Bayard Rustin, who was the organizer of the March on Washington; James Baldwin; Ella Baker, who founded the Student Nonviolent Coordinating Committee; Fannie Lou Hamer, who Malcolm meets up with as a voting rights activist. They connect so many different networks. Globally too: Malcolm in Cairo with [Ghanaian president, Kwame] Nkrumah, Malcolm in Tanzania. Martin Luther King is a Nobel Peace Prize winner and spends a month in India. Both Malcolm and King know Nkrumah, Malcolm from Harlem and King in Ghana having met him in 1957. They're extraordinary figures. Malcolm is the person who politicizes Muhammad Ali. So they are these global revolutionary figures and they are subversive. They are trying to transform the status quo and unless we really watch that through line and follow them we can get stuck with them as these icons where we don't understand they are both the sword and the shield."

At this point it seems clear that each man was somewhat more complex, multifaceted, and evolving than the monolithic figures that are often depicted. The question that hangs around them, though, is could either of them have achieved as much as they did if the other hadn't been there challenging them? "I think they both need each other," concludes Joseph. "They both have misapprehensions about each other and they make mistakes about each other. King thinks Malcolm is this narrow, anti-White Black nationalist. Malcolm thinks King is this bourgeois, reform-minded Uncle Tom when they start out. Neither of them are those things, so they both needed the other."

What's more, the contributions of each remain important to this day. "Dr. King is this major global political mobilizer and the way in which he frames this idea of racial justice globally is very important, and the numbers he attracts are very important," says Joseph. Meanwhile Malcolm has perhaps given us much of the vocabulary around racial justice even in the 21st century: "Malcolm is the first modern activist who is really saying Black lives matter in a really deep and definitive way and becomes the avatar of the Black Power movement."

BLACK POWER, BLACK PANTHERS

Despite the progress made by the Civil Rights Movement, many Black Americans still felt disenfranchised, leading to the rise of Black Power groups – most notably the revolutionary Black Panthers

Throughout the 1950s and early 1960s the Civil Rights Movement made huge strides towards racial equality, and yet by the mid 1960s Black people across the country still felt excluded from meaningful influence. Millions were debarred from political representation as well as quality education and employment opportunities. A middle-class lifestyle seemed a million miles away. The American Dream was not their reality. Frustrated with the status quo, many turned to 'Black Power'.

This term has a long history, and a variety of definitions, though it took on a very specific meaning when evolving into a public slogan during the March Against Fear in June 1966. James Meredith, the first African American to gain admission to the University of Mississippi and a man Martin Luther King Jr. described as a hero of the Civil Rights Movement, began a solitary march from Memphis, Tennessee, to Jackson, Mississippi, in a bid to encourage Black American voter registration. Two others marched with him.

On the second day of the march a White sniper called James Aubrey Norvell opened fire and hit Meredith in the shoulder. Outraged, members of the Southern Christian Leadership Conference, the Congress of Racial Equality (CORE), and the Student Nonviolent Coordinating Committee (SNCC) rallied behind Meredith's cause and the likes of King, Stokely Carmichael, and Floyd McKissick were joined by hundreds more as they completed the march.

And it was during this march, after he was arrested and held in jail for six hours, that Stokely Carmichael stirred up a crowd in Greenwood, Mississippi, declaring, "We want Black Power!" This was the first time this phrase had been engaged as a public rallying call, its use by Carmichael a battle cry for violent resistance to White oppression. It chimed with many. "When you talk about Black Power you talk about bringing this country to its knees any

time it messes with the Black man," Carmichael said later.

Initially, the SNCC and CORE had been strong exponents of nonviolent resistance, though many of their members felt that the times were changing. And when Carmichael succeeded to the chairmanship of the SNCC prior to the Meredith march, he advocated change. It appears that he had only ever regarded nonviolence as a temporary measure, not a key tenet of his belief. His move towards a call for armed resistance caused King much concern.

King believed that "the slogan was an unwise choice" and he tried to dilute its provocativeness, writing that "the Negro is powerless" and should therefore seek "to amass political and economic power to reach his legitimate goals." Carmichael, however, disagreed, and with both the SNCC and CORE repudiating nonviolence, huge ruptures emerged within the Civil Rights Movement. Like King, organizations such as the Southern Christian Leadership Conference and the National Association for the Advancement of Colored People rejected Black Power and violent protest.

On the other side, dozens of different organizations sprung up in support of Black Power, though neither Carmichael nor any other Black Power proponents offered a coherent and organized route to achieving its goals. Many young Black people knew that they wanted to mobilize and to fight for their rights but they saw no structured solutions. How would they mobilize? What exactly should they do? Into this void stepped Huey Newton and Bobby Seale. In October

At the 1968 Olympics, medallists Tommie Smith and John Carlos raised their arms in the Black Power salute

Huey Newton

The co-founder of the Black Panthers was jailed for killing Officer Frey, his incarceration becoming a rallying call for activists. He was released after three years. As the movement petered out he instead turned to drug use and died during a drug deal in 1989.

Bobby Seale

The co-founder of the Black Panthers, Seale served a four-year prison sentence for inciting a riot in Chicago during 1968 and was tried again in 1970 in a case focused on the torture and murder of fellow Panther, Alex Rackley.

Stokely Carmichael

By the time Stokely Carmichael was elected chairman of the SNCC in May 1966, he advocated violent resistance. He eventually joined the Panthers though he was at loggerheads with other party leaders who sought bonds with anti-imperialist Whites.

Eldridge & Kathleen Cleaver

Eldridge Cleaver and his wife Kathleen fled police harassment and set up a Panther branch in Algeria. After falling out with Newton, they went on to form the Revolutionary People's Communication Network.

Robert F. Williams

Williams' book, *Negroes with Guns*, detailed his experience with violent racism and his disagreement with the nonviolent wing of the Civil Rights Movement following the attacks visited upon him in Monroe. The text was a big influence on Newton.

1966, just four months after the Meredith march and Carmichael's provocative speech, Newton and Seale formed the Black Panther Party for Self-Defense. The pair had come together years earlier in the Revolutionary Action Movement (RAM), a Marxist Black organization vehemently opposed to what it regarded as American imperialism.

It was from RAM that they drew the idea, which was pivotal to Black Panther politics, that Black America was a colony within the country, and the struggle against racism was part of the global anti-colonial struggle against imperialism. RAM did not consider Black Americans citizens of the US; they were an independent nation that had been colonized on its shores. They identified strongly with the Vietnamese and were at the forefront of opposition to the Vietnam War.

RAM's honorary chair-in-exile Robert F. Williams, the author of *Negroes with Guns*, had been a member of the National Association for the Advancement of Colored People, though he took up arms to protect himself from racist violence in Monroe, North Carolina. To escape prosecution, and also a potential lynching, Williams took refuge in Cuba.

The group's influence on Newton and Seale was profound, though the two men were aware of the group's limitations. Most members of RAM were intellectuals, rather than practical activists, and they offered few solutions to how their doctrine could mobilize young Blacks in America. Newton and Seale eventually severed their ties with RAM and hit upon a way of standing up for their rights.

Throughout 1966 racial tensions were rising in their hometown of Oakland, and in the state of California as a whole. When police shot 16-year-old joyrider Matthew Johnson in San Francisco in September, Newton and Seale decided the situation had become untenable. They would protect their neighborhoods with patrols. A scheme called the Community Alert Patrol had already emerged in Watts in the aftermath of the infamous 1965 riot, whereby activists would monitor police patrols. They even sported an image of a panther on their vehicles. The vital difference for Newton and Seale, however, was that their patrols would be armed.

A teacher gets his class to raise their hands in support of Black Power

Black Panther supporters rally outside Alameda County Courthouse as Newton goes back on trial in 1970

During the remainder of 1966 the Black Panthers made several stands against the police, citing local ordinances and the Second Amendment, asserting their rights to carry arms in their vehicles as long as the weapons were not concealed. And yet the group's membership remained quite small. However, all that changed in the following year, in the wake of a number of shootings of Black men by police in North Richmond, most notably the suspected murder of Denzil Dowell.

Despite contradictory evidence, a White jury vindicated the officers' actions in the Dowell case and many residents of North Richmond began looking to the Panthers for support, bringing their own weapons to rallies and pledging their allegiance to Newton and Seale. "They had organized the rage of a Black community," says one prominent writer on the subject, "into a potent political force."

The Panthers' influence began to spread outside the state of California during the summer of 1967 when in response to earlier incidents between the Panthers and the police, the state legislature introduced a bill seeking to outlaw the carrying of loaded firearms in public. In May, 30 armed and uniformed Panthers arrived at the State Capitol building in Sacramento in order to protest against the bill. A number of them

THE SLAYING OF HAMPTON AND CLARK

Chicago in 1969 was simmering with tension. The city's police force waged a campaign against the Panthers and there were numerous reports of police brutality. One Panther, Jake Winters, took a famous stand, shooting dead two officers and injuring eight more before he was gunned down. This was the backdrop to the Fred Hampton attack on December 4. The Panthers were angry, but the law enforcement agencies wanted revenge; they would step up their operations.

The FBI had already planted informant William O'Neal into the Chicago chapter, where he was appointed the Panthers' chief of security, and during November he supplied the Bureau with detailed information about the movements of Chicago chapter leader Fred Hampton. He also provided them with a detailed map of Hampton's apartment. At 4:30 a,m, on December 4, a group of 14 officers gathered outside Hampton's home. They did not carry their usual weapons of intimidation – tear gas and sound equipment – these officers carried a submachine gun, five shotguns, a rifle and several high-caliber handguns. They had a very specific mission in mind.

Black Panther Fred Hampton, ca 1968

Their assault was executed with precision. By 4:45 a.m. Hampton lay dead in his bed, shot twice in the head, once in the arm and shoulder. He was 21 years old. Fellow Panther leader Mark Clark, 17, was also killed. Seven other Panthers in the apartment – four of whom carried bullet wounds – were arrested on charges of attempted murder, aggravated battery, and unlawful use of weapons.

And yet, according to the findings of the federal grand jury, 90 bullets were fired inside the apartment of which one came from a Panther. *The New York Times* visited the apartment and noted that while the areas where the dead Panthers had slept were clustered with bullet holes and shotgun gouges, "There were no bullet marks in the area of the two doors through which the police said they entered." In spite of all the evidence, no officers were ever charged with the murders of Hampton and Clark. O'Neal received a $300 bonus.

"A WAVE OF BLACK UPRISINGS CRASHED ACROSS THE NATION… REBELLION RE-EMERGED AS AN ACT OF POLITICAL EXPRESSION"

were arrested, and the bill passed, although it proved a PR coup for the Panthers. The press coverage was intense and thousands of young Black people across the country became aware not only of the Panthers, but of their message of armed resistance. By the end of May 1967, the Panthers had a keen membership dedicated to revolutionary ideals.

And then came the 'long, hot summer' of 1967. A wave of Black uprisings crashed across the nation and for the first time since the urban revolts during World War II, rebellion re-emerged as an act of political expression. There were many different groups espousing Black Power, though it was the Black Panthers that moved to place themselves in the vanguard.

The Panthers' first moves were cautious, historians noting that when the party

In 1969, Stokely Carmichael quit the Panthers and left the US for Guinea, where he worked for pan-African unity

published its ten-point program in the second issue of *The Black Panther* newspaper at the start of the summer, it seemed as though it was trying to explain itself, using language that lacked the confidence that should have been commensurate with its expanding influence nationwide. Yet as rioting spread, the Panthers' confidence started to grow. One of the new recruits was Eldridge Cleaver, a writer and key figure in the Black Power movement who had played a role in recruiting the Panthers as armed bodyguards for Malcolm X's widow, Betty Shabazz, early in the group's formation.

Cleaver became an important member of the party and in its nascent years used his connections to forge alliances with other left-leaning and Black Power groups. It was Newton, though, the Panthers' minister of defense, who was the key player. As the Panthers' influence spread it was Newton who members regarded as the true leader. It is hardly surprising then, that when Newton was arrested on suspicion of the murder of Officer John Frey on October 28, his release became the party's primary focus.

The 'Free Huey!' campaign attracted more press attention and when the police responded with brutal ferocity against protesters during October 1967's 'Stop the Draft Week', many leftists took up the campaign, seeing it as yet another way to protest against American imperialism. In early 1968, the party's influence really began to blossom when the Panthers announced a merger with the SNCC. And then, a few months later, everything changed.

The assassination of Martin Luther King Jr. in April 1968 saw another conflagration of racial violence ravage the country. Two days later, during a shootout between Panthers and cops in Oakland, an unarmed 17-year-old, the Panthers' national treasurer Lil' Bobby Hutton, was gunned down. The political establishment went on to appropriate King as a martyr for American democracy, but the Panthers now had Hutton as their own martyr and tens of thousands of young Black Americans mobilized in support of the party's cause. White support grew, too; Marlon Brando was one of the mourners at Hutton's funeral. Newton, meanwhile, was cast in the role of a political prisoner, incarcerated for his radical views.

By the December of 1968, the party had grown to such a size that it had offices in 20 cities all across the country. With Newton directing proceedings from his jail cell, the party also developed an intelligent strategy towards armed struggle. They remained an overt operation and did not direct their members to go on the offensive against the police. However, by stating that their members should arm themselves and should fire on any law enforcers seeking to enter their homes without a warrant, they were creating the conditions that could lead to firefights. By the end of the year, the Panthers had emerged as the most powerful Black movement in the country.

The Panthers used their growing influence to help their communities and in January 1969, began the first of their Free Breakfast for School Children programs at St. Augustine's Church in Oakland. By the end of the year, the Panthers had set up kitchens in cities across the nation, feeding over 10,000 children

A toddler and party members giving Black Panther salute

The Black Panther headquarters in Harlem circa 1970

every day before they went to school.

The government was concerned. As early as August 1967, the FBI launched COINTELPRO, a program designed to neutralize what the Bureau described as "Black nationalist hate groups." In September 1968, as more and more Panther chapters opened across America, FBI director J. Edgar Hoover dubbed the Black Panthers "the greatest threat to the internal security of the country." Over the next few years the federal government and local police forces launched a concerted attack on the Panthers, regularly feeding defamatory stories to the press, wiretapping offices, and recruiting informers.

The FBI tried to create rifts within the party, leading to internal violence and deaths, and it appointed agent provocateurs in a bid to encourage the Panthers into large-scale public attacks. They even sought to undermine the breakfast program. On occasion, they simply attacked Panther chapters, shooting up the offices and making multiple arrests. Aggression

> The Black Panther Party for Self-Defense shortened its name to the Black Panther Party in 1968

MOVE ON OVER OR WE'LL MOVE ON OVER YOU

Early Black Panthers poster, circa 1966

"THE PANTHERS HAD SET UP KITCHENS IN CITIES ACROSS THE NATION, FEEDING OVER 10,000 CHILDREN EVERY DAY"

View of protesters gathered for an 'Avenge Fred Hampton' rally, held at Boston Common, 1970

View of a line of Black Panther Party members as they stand outside the New York City courthouse

against the Panthers saw the emergence of the first SWAT team, wearing flak jackets and assault rifles. Sometimes, officers gunned down Panthers in cold blood, Fred Hampton is a case in point.

One of the FBI's key moves was to incite tension between the Panthers and the Black nationalist group Organization Us, which culminated in the shooting of Panther captain Bunchy Carter and deputy minister John Huggins on the UCLA campus in January 1969. Another firefight between the two groups in March resulted in the deaths of two more Panthers. It's ironic that state repression and agitation only boosted party membership. By the end of 1970 almost 70 different cities had Panther chapters.

For all the FBI's efforts, it was internal as well as external forces that initiated the Panthers' decline. A broader membership over an ever-expanding geographical area made it more difficult for the party to enforce its rules. The Panthers were forced into a number of purges and there are some shocking examples of

in-group torture and murder – such as that perpetrated against Alex Rackley – as the group sought to identify and oust informants. Inter-party altercations and dissent began to increase, some of which was fostered by the FBI.

> **The American far-left, anti-racist, White Panther Party formed in 1968, in response to a call from Newton**

Yet arguably the greatest obstacle to the Panthers' continued rise was the slate of concessions introduced by the government throughout 1970. President Nixon scaled back the draft and the anti-war sentiment gained further mainstream support. Black people began to enjoy more social access and political representation, while the overseas governments that had forged links with the Panthers entered into discussion with the US government. The party was quickly beginning to lose its raison d'etre.

By September 1971, the Black Panther Party had started to disintegrate, though it would remain active for many years to come. By mid 1972 it had contracted to become a local Oakland organization once more. A slow and often undignified demise followed before the Panthers finally closed their final office in 1982.

Smith's winning time of 19.8 seconds beat his own world record; it was the first time a 200-meters athlete had run under 20 seconds

Carlos and Smith were suspended from the national team and banned from the Olympic Village

© Getty

BLACK POWER SALUTE

Two black-gloved fists made an Olympic protest that reverberated around the world

Standing on the podium at the 1968 Olympic Games should have been the happiest moment in the lives of Tommie Smith and John Carlos. The two American athletes had just won the gold and bronze medals in the 200 meters in Mexico City's Olympic Stadium; Smith had broken the world record in his victory. However, instead of smiling and waving at the crowd, the athletes chose to drop their heads and hold aloft a black-gloved fist during their national anthem.

It was a political protest designed to shock the world. Smith and Carlos's salute was interpreted as a gesture of solidarity with the growing Black Power movement. Despite winning new freedoms in the Civil Rights and Voting Rights Acts of 1964 and 1965, many Black Americans felt they were still treated unfairly and discriminated against.

A great deal of thought went into the protest. Smith and Carlos wore no shoes to symbolize poverty. Carlos unzipped his tracksuit top in solidarity with blue-collar workers and wore a rosary-style necklace in memory of victims of racial murder. Both wore badges bearing the emblem of the Olympic Project for Human Rights, as did silver medallist Peter Norman, a White Australian who was aware that Smith and Carlos were going to protest on the podium. Not everything went to plan. Smith and Carlos intended to wear gloves on both hands, but Carlos forgot his so they shared Smith's pair, meaning that the athletes raised opposite hands.

The gesture made headlines around the world. The silent protest was viewed as anti-American and traitorous by many in their homeland, although the rest of the world tended to view it more sympathetically. Smith and Carlos were expelled from the US Olympic team and returned home to a torrent of abuse and death threats. Ostracized by the athletics establishment, Smith embarked on an unspectacular career in American football. Carlos continued on the track for another year, equalling the 100 yards world record, before joining Smith playing American football.

Though both suffered personally, Smith and Carlos say they have no regrets about their roles in the most famous act of political protest in a sporting arena.

President Obama presents Angelou with the Presidential Medal of Freedom

Constance Good (as Maya) stands at a lectern in a scene from the made-for-TV movie adaptation of I Know Why the Caged Bird Sings, directed by Fielder Cook, 1978. Angelou and Leonora Thuna wrote the screenplay

© Alamy, Getty

I KNOW WHY THE CAGED BIRD SINGS

Maya Angelou's bestselling book I Know Why the Caged Bird Sings was the first of a seven-part series of autobiographies, boldly telling the heartbreaking truths of her childhood and how she discovered her love of literature

By 1968, aged 40, Maya Angelou had already had many careers, including journalist, composer, civil rights worker, and educator. Following the assassination of her friend, Martin Luther King Jr., the writer James Baldwin inspired her to write a memoir so she could talk openly about her own struggles with racism as a way of dealing with grief.

The prologue of *I Know Why the Caged Bird Sings* describes a humiliating event at church when Angelou was a young child. The story then begins in 1931, when three-year-old Maya and her older brother Bailey are sent to live with their mother in Stamps, Arkansas, where the racism is overt and impacts Maya's everyday life in many ways. Years later, her father arrives unexpectedly, taking her and Bailey to Missouri to live with their mother. There, her mother's boyfriend rapes her when she is eight years old, and is killed shortly afterwards. Maya blames herself and becomes mute for several years. After returning to Stamps, she is gradually encouraged to speak again by engaging with books and poetry and reading aloud.

After enduring several appalling racist incidents in Stamps, Maya returns to live with her mother in California, where she also spends time with her father and has several experiences pivotal in her development. After having sex ("an empty night") when she is 16, Maya becomes pregnant. On Bailey's advice, she keeps it a secret until she has graduated high school. The book ends with Maya beginning to feel confident in her new role as a mother.

I Know Why the Caged Bird Sings was an immediate bestseller, nominated for a National Book Award in 1970 and staying on the *New York Times* bestseller list for two years. Angelou was hailed as a new kind of memoirist as one of the first African-American women to write about their life. As Hilton Als explained in *The New Yorker*: "She wrote about blackness from the inside, without apology or defense."

The book has faced some issues with censorship over the years, and has been removed from some school libraries following parents' complaints about explicit language and depictions of sex and violence. Despite this, *I Know Why the Caged Bird Sings* remains popular into the 21st century, and is widely considered to be a literary canon.

★★★★★★★

Audience members at Woodstock Festival, August 17, 1969

Promotional poster for the 1969
Woodstock Music and Arts Fair

JIMI HENDRIX AT WOODSTOCK

The closing act at the legendary 1969 Woodstock Music Festival, Jimi Hendrix's performance was one of the iconic moments of the 1960s

t's the morning of August 18, 1969, and tens of thousands of bleary-eyed revellers are gathered in a field to hear the closing concert of Woodstock. Jimi Hendrix, heavily sleep deprived, wearing a pink headband and wielding his signature white Fender Stratocaster, takes to the stage to deliver one of the most iconic live sets of the 20th century.

Held at a farm in upstate New York, Woodstock was one of the pivotal moments in the 1960s counterculture, attracting upwards of 400,000 people. The festival encapsulated many of the ideals of the era, its poster promoting '3 days of peace and music', yet it became equally known for its chaotic organization, technical problems, and difficult weather conditions. The line-up featured a stellar roster of rock and folk acts including Janis Joplin, Joan Baez, Jefferson Airplane, and the Grateful Dead. While he had originally been scheduled to play on Sunday night, Hendrix's performance was pushed to Monday morning at 9 a.m., when the majority of festival goers had already left. It was the only time in his career he had played so early, and at close to two hours, it was also the longest set of his career.

Following the break-up of his original band, the Jimi Hendrix Experience, two months previously, Hendrix played with a hastily assembled group of musicians he named Gypsy Sun and Rainbows. It still included long-standing drummer Mitch Mitchell, but replaced bassist Noel Redding with his old army friend Billy Cox and featured two percussionists, Juma Sultan and Jerry Velez. The band charged through many of the tracks that had made Hendrix a star, including 'Spanish Castle Magic', 'Fire', and 'Voodoo Chile'.

But it was his performance of the 'The Star Spangled Banner' that stunned the audience. Heavily drenched in feedback and distortion – which many claimed to emulate the sound of falling bombs – his rendition of the US national anthem was an era-defining moment: it mirrored a country beset by turmoil, its mythology of freedom buried beneath the violent upheavals of the Civil Rights Movement and the destruction of the war in Vietnam.

Shirley Chisholm reviewing
political statistics in 1965

A Shirley Chisholm presidential campaign poster, 1972

SHIRLEY CHISHOLM RUNS FOR PRESIDENT

The former teacher's presidential bid provided a color-coded roadmap for a future president

Shirley St. Hill was born in New York City in 1924 to West Indian parents. After graduating from college she would go on to teach elementary education, however, having been inspired by her father's support for Marcus Garvey, following her marriage to Conrad Chisholm in 1949, she immersed herself in politics and to fighting racism and sexism.

By 1964, she had been elected to the New York State Assembly, and achieved improved unemployment benefits and education for underprivileged students. In 1968 she became the first Black woman in Congress. Focusing on nutrition programs for the disenfranchised, Chisholm only hired women, 50 percent of whom were Black. With values instilled by her grandmother, she rose to party leadership, while prize-winning debating skills enabled her to serve seven terms from 1969.

Chisholm co-founded the Congressional Black Caucus in 1971 after debuting her 1970 autobiography *Unbought and Unbossed* (signalling her congressional campaign slogan). She became the first Black candidate to run for a major party's nomination for president and the first woman to run for the Democratic Party's presidential nomination in the 1972 US presidential election.

However, paving the way for the likes of Barack Obama and Hillary Clinton in 2008 was dangerous. Death threats saw Chisholm require Secret Service protection. Still, wide-ranging support propelled her to become the first woman to appear in a US presidential debate. However, sexism, skepticism, and an underfunded campaign saw Chisholm finish fourth behind George McGovern. She retired in 1983 to teach and care for her second husband. In 1993 she was inducted into the National Women's Hall of Fame. The Shirley Chisholm Project maintains a legacy sealed by a 'forever stamp' of approval from the US Postal Service honoring her in 2014, while in 2015, President Barack Obama posthumously awarded Chisholm the Presidential Medal of Freedom. In 2019, the first sections of the Shirley Chisholm State Park opened.

Uzo Aduba's award-winning portrayal of Chisholm in the 2020 miniseries *Mrs. America* portrayed a pioneering candidate of the people. Both Danai Gurira and Regina King are slated to play her in upcoming biopics. The pandemic may have delayed the erection of a monument honoring Chisholm, who died aged 80 in 2005, but she can never be erased from history.

RUMBLE IN THE JUNGLE

The famous boxing extravaganza in Zaire that relaunched the legend of Muhammad Ali

The hype for the heavyweight championship boxing match in October 1974 was huge, but the result was not supposed to be in doubt. Undisputed champion George Foreman was defending his titles against Muhammad Ali, himself a former champion. Foreman had 40 wins and no losses on his record. Ali had become embroiled in a legal battle to overturn his conviction for draft evasion, citing his religious beliefs and ethical opposition to the Vietnam War, and did not fight for four years. His comeback looked destined to fail after defeats to Joe Frazier and Ken Norton.

Nevertheless, promoter Don King knew that Ali was still a crowd-pleaser. He sweet-talked Foreman and Ali into agreeing a bout if he could guarantee each of them a $5 million payday. Zaire's dictatorial leader Mobutu Sese Seko agreed to fund the purse after he was persuaded that the publicity created by hosting such a high-profile sporting event would boost his autocratic regime.

The boxers spent the summer of 1974 training in Zaire and met in Kinshasa's Stade du 20 Mai, once a site where dissidents were executed, on October 30. After both fighters traded blows in the first round, Ali suddenly switched tactics. In what he later dubbed his rope-a-dope plan, Ali leaned back on the ropes and allowed Foreman to punch his arms and body. While Ali soaked up the battering, Foreman's energy was sapped for little reward.

Ali countered where possible, taunting Foreman by whispering in his ear, "They told me you could punch, George!" By the eighth round, Ali landed a combination that culminated in a left hook and a straight right-hander to the face. Foreman fell to the canvas and, although he got up again, was counted out before he was upright.

It was not just a sporting triumph; it was a financial success, too. The bout was watched by an estimated one billion people, one-quarter of the world's population, and raised $100 million in revenue. It was a defining moment in the career of Muhammad Ali, a boxer who would go on to become one of sport's most iconic figures.

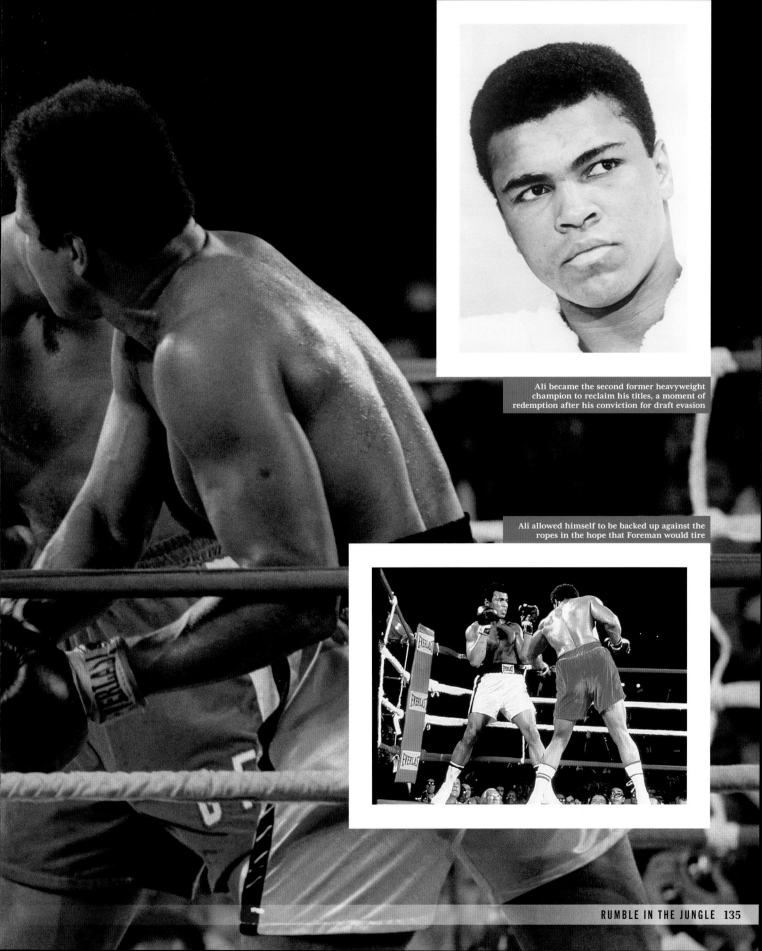

Ali became the second former heavyweight champion to reclaim his titles, a moment of redemption after his conviction for draft evasion

Ali allowed himself to be backed up against the ropes in the hope that Foreman would tire

THE RISE OF HIP HOP

Hip hop music and culture has become one of the most far-reaching and influential movements of the 20th century and beyond

Hip hop culture began in the Bronx, New York City, in the early 1970s – an area mainly inhabited by Black Americans, Latino Americans, and Caribbean immigrants.

Although sometimes used to describe rap music, the term 'hip hop' actually refers to an all-encompassing culture made up of four key elements: DJing, or 'turntabling' – music made with record players and mixers; MCing, or 'rhyming' – a rhythmic and rhyming vocal style; B-boying, or breakdancing – encompassing movement, dance, style and attitude; and graffiti, also known as 'writing'. There is sometimes a fifth element added to the list, especially by artists and scholars who consider themselves socially conscious, and that is 'knowledge', referring to a certain kind of street knowledge, awareness of historical roots and 'realness' that the hip hop culture aspires to.

THE BEGINNING

In the early 1970s, against a backdrop of the glitzy disco scene happening in the wealthier areas of New York City, Black people in the Bronx were hosting DJ parties, playing predominantly Black-made funk and soul records. Here, the art forms of DJing, dancing, and rapping evolved alongside each other. DJ Kool Herc, an 18-year-old Jamaican immigrant, blew people's minds at a now legendary house party in 1973 when he used two turntables (and two copies of the same record) to meld together the percussive breaks of dance tracks, creating a continuous flow of music. This innovation inspired an explosion of improvisational dancing and soon contests developed at which 'breakdancing' – a dazzling combination of acrobatic and sometimes airborne moves, complete with gravity-defying headspins – was born.

DJ Herc, along with two other pioneers – Afrika Bambaataa and Grandmaster Flash – form what some people refer to as 'the Holy Trinity' of hip hop history. They were among the first to isolate and extend the break beat, laying the foundation for the hip hop beats we know today. In 1973, Bambaataa, a Bronx-born son of Caribbean activists, formed Zulu Nation with a group of gang members who wanted to turn their lives around. Together they brought the community together through music. Meanwhile, over on the south side of the Bronx, son of Barbadian immigrants, Grandmaster Flash was perfecting the art form – after studying other DJs' techniques and the experimentation as a teenager. He added style to DJing, connecting groundbreaking technique with technical knowledge to make the turntables into an instrument. At these early parties, it was common for the DJs to have a microphone where they would say things to the crowd to get people pumped up. Grandmaster Flash found it difficult to speak while DJing, so he started leaving a microphone out for others.

RAP, 'SCRATCH' & INFLUENCES

The young people picking up those microphones at parties were likely influenced by the musical and cultural icons who are now recognized as central to the formation of hip hop. One of these was the boxer Muhammad Ali, who in 1963 released a comedy spoken-word album, demonstrating his unique poetic 'trash talk'. I Am the Greatest included some of the rhymes Ali would often recite before his fights.

The Last Poets, a collective of spoken-word artists who performed on the New York television program Soul! in 1968, released their debut self-titled album in 1970. In 1971, the jazz poet and soul singer Gil Scott-Heron released Pieces of a Man. The record features classic tracks such

Gil Scott-Heron (1949-2011), one of hip hop's early influences, performing in February 1976

Grandmaster Flash, DJ Kool Herc, Afrika Bambaataa, and Chuck D pose at Columbia University's Rap Summit in New York City, 1993

as 'The Revolution Will Not Be Televised', a beautifully rhythmic critique of mass media and governments.

Other musicians often identified as influencing elements of hip hop include the 1950s rock 'n' roll pioneer, Bo Diddley; 1960s funk legend, James Brown, and the entertainer Pigmeat Markham, particularly his 1968 single, 'Here Comes the Judge'.

In 1975, Kool Herc was hired to play music at the Hevalo Club in the Bronx and got his friend Coke La Rock to deliver crowd-pleasing rhymes ("DJ Riz is in the house and he'll turn it out without a doubt"). The same year, Grand Wizzard Theodore was trying to hold a spinning record in place so he could hear what his mother was shouting at him, and accidentally caused the record to produce the 'shigi-shigi' sound now known as 'the scratch'.

THE 1977 BLACKOUT

A blackout affected most of New York City over two days in July 1977, resulting in widespread looting. Following the blackout there was no shortage of mixers, turntables, and speakers in the Bronx. At the time, the hip hop genre was still barely known outside of the area, but following the blackout its reach and popularity began to grow at an extraordinary rate.

Although the word 'rap' (meaning 'converse'), had been used in African-American Vernacular English (AAVE) for decades (along with 'hip', from the Wolof verb 'hepi' meaning 'to see'), it wasn't widely known until the years following the 1977 blackout. It was around this time the music industry coined the term 'rap music' and the focus shifted away from DJs and towards MCs.

Grandmaster Flash, focusing intently on the turntables while performing, circa 1980

De La Soul's early releases were characterized by witty, innovative lyrics and creative sampling

> ## "FOLLOWING THE BLACKOUT THERE WAS NO SHORTAGE OF MIXERS, TURNTABLES, AND SPEAKERS IN THE BRONX"

OLD SCHOOL

The term 'old-school hip hop' generally refers to the first commercially recorded hip hop music – approximately 1979 to 1983. Before this, the music had been performed live or occasionally recorded on tapes from PA systems and then distributed at parties.

In 1979, The Sugarhill Gang's 'Rapper's Delight' – which is now widely regarded as the first rap hit – reached number 36 on the Billboard Charts. The same year, Grandmaster Flash formed supergroup the Furious Five, who went on to become one of the most influential rap outfits ever. By this time, hip hop had spread from the confines of New York City, and in 1979, Lady B in Philadelphia became the first female solo hip hop artist to commercially record music with her single 'To the Beat Y'All' – which went on to became a stock rap phrase.

In 1980, after meeting hip hop pioneers like Fab 5 Freddy, Blondie released their hit single 'Rapture', which was the first number-one

Public Enemy performing in Hamburg, Germany in 2000

Run-DMC hit the mainstream after teaming up with rock group Aerosmith on 'Walk This Way'

single in the US to feature rap-style vocals. In 1982, Grandmaster Flash and the Furious Five released their single 'The Message'. Now widely regarded as one of the most important tracks in hip hop history, 'The Message' provides social commentary on inner-city poverty, with hooks such as "It's like a jungle sometimes, it makes me wonder / How I keep from going under," the genre makes a shift from party to protest and lays the foundations for conscious hip hop.

A NEW SOUND

The second wave of hip hop in the early 1980s, known as 'new school', was still predominantly being made in New York City. It was characterized by drum machine-led sampler technology, and introduced artists like Run-DMC and LL Cool J, who exuded a tough, cool, street b-boy image and attitude, with boastful self-assertive raps. While acts like KRS-One and Chuck D continued on the route of socio-political commentary, combining hip hop with pro-Black activism.

In 1984, Russell Simmons and Rick Rubin launched the hip hop label Def Jam Recordings, releasing 'It's Yours' by T La Rock & Jazzy Jay, followed by 'I Need a Beat' by LL Cool J. Both tracks sold well, leading to a distribution deal with CBS Records through

Ice Cube and Eazy-E of NWA performing in Chicago, 1989, as part of the 'Straight Outta Compton' tour

Columbia Records. That year at the Grammy Awards, Michael Jackson borrowed elements of b-boy dance moves he'd seen performed by LA breakdancers, showing off his now infamous 'moonwalk'.

THE GOLDEN AGE

Hip hop music produced between the mid-1980s and the mid-1990s is referred to as the 'golden age'. With sample-heavy music dominating the

scene, many of the albums released during this time period wouldn't have received legal clearance today.

Afrocentrism and political militancy are lyrical themes associated with the era. In 1987, Public Enemy stunned the world with their debut album Yo! Bum Rush the Show. Although largely ignored by radio stations, due to controversy around its radically pro-Black lyrical content, the politically charged album went on to become one of the fastest-selling hip hop records, selling 400,000 copies in the US by 1989.

The golden age is known for its innovation and was described by Rolling Stone as a time "when it seemed that every new single reinvented the genre." Artists associated with the era include De La Soul, Gang Starr, A Tribe Called Quest, and Pete Rock and CL Smooth. In 1988, MTV launched a new hip hop show called Yo! MTV Raps.

GANGSTA RAP

Schoolly D's 1985 single 'P.S.K. What Does It Mean?' is often considered to be the first gangsta rap song, followed by Ice-T's '6 in the Mornin'', from 1986.

In the early days of the golden age, gangsta rap hit the mainstream with NWA's pioneering gold album Straight Outta Compton (1988), which featured the track 'F**k tha Police'. Their second album, N****z4Life, followed in 1991 and was the first hardcore rap album to reach number one on the pop charts. The group's explicit lyrics, which were often misogynistic and hinted at homophobic and anti-Semitic sentiments, saw them banned from mainstream radio stations. Despite this, several members of the original lineup, such as Dr. Dre, Eazy-E, and Ice Cube, went on to become platinum-selling solo artists in the 1990s.

The gangsta rap subgenre was male-dominated and often featured misogynistic lyrics, with music videos that sexualized and

The creativity and innovation of hip hop has inspired new scenes all over the globe

Hip hop culture formed from a DIY approach and an attitude of resistance against authority – a message and energy that has resonated with, and appealed to, people all around the world.

Caribbean and Latin American people played an integral part in the early development of hip hop in the Bronx, so it's no surprise that the style and culture spread to almost every country in those regions, such as Haiti, Cuba, and Brazil. Just as with the US, in many Latin American and Caribbean countries hip hop has been a tool in which the Afro-descendant population can celebrate their blackness and articulate their demands for racial equality. Reggaeton is a style of music developed in Puerto Rico that has a lot of similarities with US-based hip hop, both being influenced by Jamaican music and incorporating rapping and call and response.

It's also possible to find vibrant hip hop scenes all over Europe, Africa, and Asia, with UK hip hop becoming a genre all of its own, with many new subgenres such as garage and grime. Notable artists from the UK scene include Dizzee Rascal, The Streets, Ms. Dynamite, Foreign Beggars, MIA, Akala, Lowkey, Lady Leshurr, and Stormzy. In the 1990s in France, Senegalese-born MC Solaar became the first non-American rap superstar.

Every October in Braunschweig, Germany, 3,500 hip hop fans from around the world attend the biggest global hip hop dance competition, the Battle of the Year. Elimination competitions for the event are held in 20 different countries around the world. In Kenya, young rappers tend to speak in 'sheng', a creolized language that includes English, Swahili, and Kikuyu words, and rap about joblessness, poverty, and failures of the older generation. There are lively and growing scenes in China ('xi ha') and Ghana ('hip-life'), as well as in Sweden, Norway, New Zealand, Chile, Indonesia, and many other countries worldwide.

Contestants perform at a regional elimination round in China, for the 2005 Battle of the Year hip hop dance contest

Kendrick Lamar performing in Boston in 2017 on the 'DAMN' tour

objectified women. This disregard for female voices and perspective grew to define much of mainstream hip hop, with the recording industry often placing emphasis on female rappers' sexuality over their artistic abilities – if they were willing to back them at all.

GOING MAINSTREAM

It was in 1990 that hip hop music really hit the mainstream, in part due to the success of Public Enemy's album, *Fear of a Black Planet*, which was met by rave reviews. In 1991, Cypress Hill released their self-titled debut, selling two million copies in the US alone, and following up with a second album (*Black Sunday*) in 1993, which went straight to number one on the Billboard 200. Also in 1993, Dr. Dre's debut from the previous year, *The Chronic*, attained multi-platinum status.

Other hip hop albums that burst into the mainstream in the early 1990s include: MC Hammer's 1990 release Please Hammer Don't Hurt 'Em; Wu Tang Clan's 1993 release, Enter the Wu-Tang (36 Chambers); and the all-female TLC's CrazySexyCool (1994), which was hugely successful, earning four top five singles including two number ones – 'Creep' and 'Waterfalls' (1995).

In 1996, The Fugees breathed new life into socially aware hip hop with The Score, which debuted at number one, almost immediately

> **"A CONFLICT ERUPTED THAT SAW MANY MEMBERS OF THE SCENE ON BOTH SIDES CAUGHT UP IN VIOLENCE"**

becoming the best-selling hip hop album of all time, and earning them two Grammys. With roots in reggae and soul, The Score has a warm and intimate sound. In 1998, Missy 'Misdemeanor' Elliott redefined hip hop and R&B further, with her first album, Supa Dupa Fly. She went on to become the highest-selling female rapper of all time.

EAST COAST VS WEST COAST

During the 1990s, a feud developed between artists and fans of the East Coast and West Coast hip hop scenes in the United States. The focal points of the rivalry were Tupac Shakur (West Coast) and his LA label Death Row Records, and the Notorious B.I.G. (East Coast) and his New York label Bad Boy Records. In 1991, Bronx rapper Tim Dog voiced his anger at record companies rejecting East Coast rappers in favor of West Coast ones on his track 'F**k Compton', which featured shots at the whole LA rap scene. From here, a conflict erupted that continued for over five years and saw many members of the scene on both sides caught up in violence. The media got involved, continuously reporting on the 'coastal rap war' in 1995-96, and fans began picking sides. The feud reached a peak when Tupac Shakur and the Notorious B.I.G. were both killed by unknown assailants, in 1996 and 1997 respectively.

BLING ERA

A new commercial hip hop sound materialized in the late 1990s, often referred to as the 'bling era' (referencing Lil Wayne's single 'Bling Bling', 1999) or sometimes the 'jiggy era' (derived from 'Gettin' Jiggy Wit It' by Will Smith, 1997). Sean 'Puff Daddy' Combs' 1997 album *No Way Out* signalled a stylistic change in gangsta rap, and mainstream hip hop generally, as it became more accepted and commercially successful. Producers of this era favored R&B-style hooks and production, often using samples of soul and pop tracks from the 1970s and 1980s, with materialistic lyrics.

However, in 1998, Lauryn Hill (from The Fugees) released her solo debut album, The Miseducation of Lauryn Hill. It incorporated several musical styles – such as neo soul, gospel, and reggae – to create a unique sound, with lyrics exploring motherhood, love, and religion. The album received critical acclaim, 11 Grammy nominations (with five wins), and left a lasting legacy. In 2018, Sony Music reported it to have sold 20 million copies worldwide. In 1999, The Neptunes (a production duo of Chad Hugo and Pharrell Williams) dominated the airwaves with a string of hit singles featuring a variety of vocalists, such as Kelis and ODB. Other pop-orientated acts of this time period include Nelly, Ja Rule, and Fabolous, while others – such as DMX, 50 Cent, G-Unit, and The Game – found success with a grittier sound. Hip hop was also influencing nu-metal artists such as Korn and Limp Bizkit, and heavily impacting mainstream pop with artists like Destiny's Child, Usher, and Erykah Badu.

ALTERNATIVE SOUND

In the early to mid 2000s, there was a resurgence of 'alternative hip hop', first introduced in the 1980s with artists such as De La Soul and The Pharcyde. The sub-genre began to find a place in the mainstream, due to acts like Gnarls Barkley, MF Doom, and Mos Def. Outkast's *Speakerboxxx/ The Love Below* (2003) appealed to a wide audience as it included elements of several other genres, including rock, R&B, punk, jazz, country, and electronica, and went on to be one of the best-selling hip hop albums of all time.

PROGRESSIVE

Sometimes termed 'the blog era', partly due to the increased use of social media and blogging for music distribution and promotion, the 'progressive' era was a continuation of the success of alternative hip hop, which was outselling gangsta rap by the late 2000s. The success of Kanye West's 2008 album *808s & Heartbreak* – full of songs about love, loneliness, and heartache – had a significant effect on hip hop, and inspired future generations. An avant-garde approach to production became popular, with wide-ranging influences from jazz, rock, and soul. Artists associated with this subgenre include Drake, Lupe Fiasco, and Kendrick Lamar.

Around this time, the popularity of Auto-Tune vocal effects increased with the rapper T-Pain. Nicknamed the 'T-Pain effect', it was a prominent fixture in late 2000s and early 2010s hip hop, used by artists such as Snoop Dogg, Lil Wayne, and the Black Eyed Peas.

THE RISE CONTINUES

From the underground beginnings of Bronx house parties, hip hop has grown into a global movement and cultural phenomenon, influencing many aspects of popular culture – such as fashion, art, theater, and radio – both in the United States and around the world. In 2017, Forbes reported that hip hop/R&B (MRC Data classified them as one genre) had taken over rock as the most consumed musical genre. In recent years, hip hop lyrics have also gained legitimacy in academic and literary circles, with studies of hip hop linguistics now offered at several institutions. Artists like Jay Z and P. Diddy have huge presences in fashion and media, as well as music, while the entrepreneurial success of many hip hop artists have gone on to inspire many young Black Americans.

There have been many subgenres added to hip hop over the years. In addition to the ones mentioned, there's also crunk, glitch-hop, country rap, emo rap, lofi hip hop, and trap, among others. In the 2020s, the storytelling rap of the past seems to be less popular and there is less emphasis on lyrical content in much of the rap that makes it into the charts. However, there are some current artists, such as Kendrick Lamar, who keep the 1990s sensibilities alive with political and emotional lyricism.

Hip hop artists all over the world are breaking down the boundaries between 'high' and 'low' art, in order to make truth-telling work to reflect their generation, and courageously leading the way towards transformation and empowerment.

Wyclef Jean, Lauryn Hill, and Pras of The Fugees in Chicago, 1996

Oprah's talk show ran in 140 countries and was on air for 25 years

President Obama awards Oprah Winfrey the Presidential Medal of Freedom in 2013

The Oprah Winfrey Leadership Academy for Girls was opened in 2007

THE OPRAH WINFREY SHOW DEBUTS

Triumphing over tragedy, this global icon turned a recurring motif into a billion-dollar business

Oprah Gail Winfrey was born into poverty in Mississippi in 1954, raised by her grandmother and mother. Faith helped her overcome molestation, teenage pregnancy, and the loss of her son.

Moving to Tennessee to live with her father saw Oprah become a popular student crowned Miss Black Tennessee, attracting a local radio job. An oratory contest win secured a scholarship to Tennessee State University to study communication. By 19, Oprah was the youngest and first Black female co-news anchor.

In 1978 Oprah co-hosted *People Are Talking*; by 1984 she was hosting 30-minute show *AM Chicago*. Within months it became the highest-rated talk show, and critic Roger Ebert persuaded her to sign a national syndication deal.

A millionaire by 32, Oprah negotiated ownership rights to *The Oprah Winfrey Show*, expanding it to an hour, and started production company HARPO. The first episode was broadcast nationally on September 8, 1986, becoming the number-one daytime talk show and the highest-rated television program of its kind. It ran for 25 years in 140 countries until May 25, 2011. Her relatable nature brought gender diversity to the genre welcoming mostly female viewers.

Celebrities flocked to Oprah's 'confessional couch'. The richest African American of the 20th century became the first Black female billionaire. Revolutionizing tabloid talk – she covered topics from literature to spirituality, alongside commercial giveaways.

Oprah's endorsement of Barack Obama in the 2008 presidential race equalled one million votes. In 2013, he awarded her the Presidential Medal of Freedom. In 2018, the National Museum of African American History and Culture launched an exhibit on Oprah's cultural influence. A University of Illinois course focuses on her business acumen.

Oprah's legacy is multi-pronged: actress, TV Producer, *O, the Oprah Magazine*, *The Oprah Show* and *Sunday Soul* weekly podcasts, and Oprah.com. In 2011, she formed OWN and launched a partnership with Apple TV+ in 2018. Her 2021 interview with the duke and duchess of Sussex had global appeal. Considering herself a teacher, The Oprah Winfrey Leadership Academy for Girls in South Africa is her most fitting gift.

★ ★ ★ ★ ★ ★ ★

RODNEY KING AND THE LA RIOTS

When four police officers were acquitted of brutally beating a Black man in 1992, despite being caught on film, decades of outrage over a racist criminal justice system finally spilled over

n 1991, a Black man named Rodney King, on parole for robbery, led police on a high-speed chase across Los Angeles. When they finally caught up with him, and Rodney got down on his hands and knees, they beat him severely for 15 minutes, in front of more than a dozen other officers – leaving him with skull fractures, broken bones, and irreversible brain damage.

With footage of the beating broadcast widely across the media, four of the officers were charged with excessive use of force. In the ensuing year, the nation watched the trial with bated breath, keenly aware that this was not merely an isolated incident – it was a test of the country's notoriously racist criminal justice system. The same month as King's beating, after mistaking a Black teenage girl for a shoplifter and killing her, a Korean shopkeeper had escaped with just a fine of $500.

So, when a jury of 12 residents – nine White, one Asian, one Latino, and one mixed race – found the officers not guilty, within just a few hours, the city erupted in outrage. Concentrated in the predominantly Black area of South Central LA, plagued with drug addiction, gang violence, and unemployment, rioters set fires to businesses, dragging White and Latino motorists from their cars and beating them.

Although LAPD Chief Darryl Gates declared the situation under control, the police were utterly unable to respond to the looting and violence for hours. On the third day of rioting, King himself issued a public appeal for calm, but it continued for two more days, leaving 50 dead, 2,000 injured, and 6,000 behind bars, as well as $1 billion of property destroyed, including 2,000 Korean businesses.

Though the curfew was eventually lifted, the flames of outrage continued to burn, bringing the long-overlooked issue of police brutality and injustice to the forefront. King was later awarded a settlement in court, while two of his attackers spent 30 months in prison and the other two were fired, and Darryl Gates was forced to resign. However, the video of the beating ended up being just the first of many police brutality cases to go viral; an issue reignited in 2020 by the death of George Floyd.

Within hours, South Central Los Angeles resembled a war zone, with businesses robbed and burned down, and police unable to respond

Reflecting growing tensions between LA's Black and ethnic Asian communities, many of the rioters targeted Korean businesses

© Getty

BARACK OBAMA: THE FIRST BLACK PRESIDENT

Barack Obama quickly became a rising star in the Democratic Party. He was an intelligent and charismatic politician, as well as a gifted communicator, capturing the imagination of the public, first as Illinois senator and later as the first Black president of the United States

Barack Obama being sworn in as 44th president of the United States, a truly momentous occasion for America and African Americans

t was a historical day on November 4, 2008, when Barack Hussein Obama II was elected the 44th President of the United States. In that important victory, Obama received 52.9 percent of the popular vote and 365 electoral votes, winning more votes than any candidate in history. He received support from a variety of groups, including 95 percent of Black American voters. The American population's decision to have their first Black president was a major step for racial reconciliation in a country tarnished by its past enslavement and segregation of Black people, and the continuing discrimination and violence against them.

Barack Obama was born on August 4, 1961, in Hawaii. He is the son of Ann Dunham, a White American from Kansas, and Barack Obama Sr., a Black Kenyan studying in the United States. The couple met at a Russian language class at the University of Hawaii and married under a year later. His parents separated and he later moved to Indonesia with his mother's new husband, where the family spent several years until Obama moved back to Hawaii and stayed partly with his mum and his maternal grandparents.

Obama left Hawaii for college, enrolling first at Occidental College in Los Angeles for his freshman and sophomore years, and then at Columbia University in New York City, where he graduated with a degree in political science in 1983. After spending an additional year in New York as a researcher at a global business consulting firm, Obama started working as a community organizer in Chicago's largely impoverished South Side. In 1988, he enrolled at the prestigious Harvard Law School, where he was elected as president of the renowned *Harvard Law Review* for the academic year 1990-91. Later reflecting on his selection as the first Black president of the *Harvard Law Review*, Obama noted in his book, *Audacity of Hope*, that the intense publicity following his victory represented what he described as "America's hunger for an optimistic sign from the racial front – a morsel of proof that after all, some progress has been made." During a summer internship at Chicago's Sidley Austin law firm after his first year at Harvard, Obama met Michelle Robinson, a South Side native and Princeton University and Harvard Law School graduate who supervised his work at the firm. The two married in 1992. After completing his law degree, Obama got involved in the Democratic Party in Chicago, where he organized Project Vote, which registered thousands of Black Americans on voting rolls.

Obama launched his first campaign for political office in 1996 after his district's state senator, Alice Palmer, decided to run for Congress. Obama announced his candidacy to replace her in the Illinois legislature and went on to be elected. Obama was able to campaign

©Getty

for finance reform and crime legislation, even when the party was in the minority. After 2002, when the Democrats won control of the Senate, he became a leading legislator, where he worked on nearly 300 bills aimed at helping children, old people, labor unions, and the poor.

Obama began preparing for the 2004 race for the US Senate seat held by Peter Fitzgerald, a first-term Republican who decided not to run for re-election. Advised by political consultant David Axelrod, who had a strong record of helping Black candidates succeed in majority-White constituencies, Obama assembled a coalition of Black Americans and White liberals to take the Democratic Senate primary in a landslide victory.

He then moved toward the political center to wage his general election campaign against Republican nominee Jack Ryan, who later was forced to drop out of the race when infamous details about his divorce were made public. Obama secured an easy victory against Ryan's replacement on the ballot, Black conservative Republican Alan Keyes. Obama won by the largest margin in the history of Senate elections in Illinois, 70 percent to 27 percent. While campaigning for the US Senate, Obama was invited to deliver the keynote address at the 2004 Democratic National Convention.

Obama working from his campaign plane destined for New York, as part of a series of fundraisers

This iconic photo shows the president and other officials receiving updates on the hunt for Osama bin Laden

Obama and his family in Chicago, after winning his second term as president

The Obama Portraits have drawn huge crowds

His famous speech (titled 'The Audacity of Hope') positioned him as the Democratic Party's rising star. In the speech, he powerfully asserted that there were no blue states or red states in America but rather the United States of America.

Two years into his first US Senate term, Obama announced he was going to explore a presidential bid on January 16, 2007, later declaring his candidacy for the US presidency on February 10, 2007 at the Old State Capitol in Illinois. After intense months of primary elections, on June 7 the earlier front-runner, Senator Hillary Clinton, was the last of the Democratic presidential challengers to concede and Obama became the first Black American to be nominated by either party, running against Republican Senator John McCain for the highest office in the country. In his nomination acceptance speech, delivered in front of 80,000 at Mile High Stadium, Obama continued the slogans of his campaign to date ("Change We Can Believe In," "Yes, We Can!") and supported them with real figures: 95 percent of Americans would see tax cuts, he will invest $150 million in renewable energy sources, within ten years Americans would no longer depend on Middle Eastern oil.

Obama won the election and in his acceptance speech in his hometown of Chicago said, "If there is anyone out there who still doubts that America is a place where all things are possible; who still wonders if the dream of our founders is alive in our time; who still questions the power of our democracy, tonight is your answer," alluding to the significance

> ## "OBAMA BECAME THE FIRST BLACK AMERICAN TO BE NOMINATED BY EITHER PARTY, RUNNING FOR THE HIGHEST OFFICE"

of his election as the first Black American president as a triumph for democracy. On January 20, 2009, hundred of thousands witnessed in person and millions around the world watched on television as Obama took the oath of office as president.

Being the US president for eight years, leaving office on January 20, 2017, Obama and his administration left behind a large legacy that was formed early on. After less than a month in office, Obama was able to sign a $787 billion economic stimulus package into law, creating an economic turnaround of the Great Recession in the US that prevented an economic catastrophe, one of his big victories during his presidency. He received the Nobel Peace Prize in 2009 for his efforts to improve relations with countries that the USA had alienated during George Bush's presidency. The Obama administration also scaled back on its troop commitments and was in charge of the operation of killing Osama bin Laden. Some of Obama's most notable achievements, such as the Affordable Care Act (Obamacare), the Paris Climate Agreement, and Deferred Action on Child Arrivals were either under attack or overturned by the following president. One important – some argue the most important – feature of Obama's presidency, though, can never be taken away: he was the first Black American president, showing the young and future generations of Americans of all skin colors and backgrounds that they have the opportunity to live in the White House and be the president of the United States.

THE OBAMA PORTRAITS

The Obama Portraits in Smithsonian's National Portrait Gallery manifests the importance of the f irst Black American president and f irst lady

From the moment the presidential portraits of Barack and Michelle Obama were unveiled at Smithsonian's National Portrait Gallery in Washington, D.C., on February 12, 2018, they have attracted millions of visitors and a large public following. Created by the internationally renowned New York-based Kehinde Wiley and Jersey City-based Amy Sherald, the first Black American artists to be commissioned to paint the official presidential portraits, the works are testimonies to the lives and power of the couple.

Wiley is well-known for his regal portraiture of contemporary Black men and women in which he uses the traditional imagery used for royalty and heroes to represent the power and dignity of the people who are often invisible on museum walls. In the portrait of Barack Obama, Wiley has placed him in an inlaid wood revival chair, citing Lincoln's portrait. He wears a suit but no tie, looking directly at the viewer and seated against a background of green foliage with flowers, representing different periods of his life and the blooming possibility his presidency symbolized for all Americans.

Sherald, known for her portraits of ordinary Black Americans from her community, portrayed the first lady as she sits in a floor-length white dress with multi-colored fields of patterns against a bold blue background, looking directly out at the viewer. Michelle Obama has perfectly summarized the importance of the portraits: "What matters most is that [the portraits are] there for young people to see – that our faces help dismantle the perception that in order to be enshrined in history, you have to look a certain way. If we belong, then so, too, can many others."

BIRTH OF THE NEW CIVIL RIGHTS MOVEMENT

Black Lives Matter has sparked the spirit of protest against the racism faced by African Americans and Black people across the globe. The new struggle mixes civil rights and the politics of Black Power

Trayvon Martin was only 17 when he was killed walking back from the shops. His killer, George Zimmerman, followed him because he looked 'suspicious', provoked a confrontation, and then shot the unarmed teenager to death. But police had to be pressured into arresting him, weeks after the event, because they believed he acted in self-defense. The

eventual trial stirred all the stereotypes of the 'Black superhuman menace', and Zimmerman was ultimately acquitted. On hearing the verdict, activist Alicia Garza wrote a Facebook post in dismay, which ended with the words "Our Lives Matter". Her friend Patrisse Cullors took this phrase and created the hashtag #BlackLivesMatter, which spread as quickly as the pain from the verdict. The killing of an unarmed Black teenager ignited the spirit

of protest not for the first or last time in American history.

Emmett Till had a profound impact on the Civil Rights Movement without ever marching, protesting, or making a speech. As a 14-year-old visiting family in Mississippi, he was lynched by a racist mob for 'disrespecting' a White woman. His mother, Mamie Till, insisted the mutilated body of her child was displayed in an open casket at the funeral. The

image sent shivers down the collective spine of America and galvanized support for the Civil Rights Movement. It is a sad testament to just how little has changed that more than 60 years later it was the killing of a Black teenager that awoke the masses.

#BlackLivesMatter was sparked by the killing of Trayvon Martin but found its platform when unarmed teenager Michael Brown was shot dead by a police officer in Ferguson, Missouri, on August 9, 2014. Protests erupted in Ferguson,

whose population was two-thirds African American, while its police force had only three Black officers in total. Michael Brown's killing was the straw that broke the camel's back in police-community relations and major periods of unrest broke out in the city through the remainder of 2014 and into 2015. Stories of police brutality, racism, and the targetting of African Americans were a reminder that many of the same problems that existed in the original civil rights struggle persist in

contemporary America. The original movement may have outlawed discrimination and segregation, while securing voting rights for African Americans, but it had not guaranteed equality before the law or her officers. Tamir Rice, Eric Garner, Philando Castile, and Korryn Gaines represent just a fraction of those killed by the police that are testament to the most fundamental form of racial injustice.

Since emancipation from slavery, African Americans have been victims of the criminal

Protests over the police shooting of Michael Brown in Ferguson, Missouri

The shooting of Alton Sterling in 2016 led the DOJ to open a civil rights investigation

justice system. One of the ways that free Black labor was retained in the South was to put prison chain gangs to work. African Americans were subject to incarceration for fines and minor offenses to ensure they would populate the chain gangs. Though being victimized by the prison system is not new; between 1980 and 2012 there was a 222 percent increase in the incarceration rate in America. The war on crack cocaine was a major factor in this steep rise, and hugely disproportionately put African Americans into prison. Almost a million African Americans spend time in prison each year, and it is estimated that there are more Black men behind bars today, or on probation and parole, than there were enslaved in 1850. Mass incarceration has become perhaps the most important civil rights issue in the 21st century. The impact of loss of liberty, voting rights, and ability to find employment led Michelle Alexander to declare the prison industry the "new Jim Crow." With around five million African Americans outside of prison under state supervision on a daily basis, the police have become ever-present in Black communities. To some they have come

to symbolize the boots on the ground of racism, the militarized storm troopers of racial injustice.

Black Lives Matter is similar to the Civil Rights Movement in that it is a banner for a number of independent organizations, which existed before the hashtag came into being. It has grown into an international organization with 40 chapters around the world. They use the same name and adopt the policy platform but are run by those who were already working on the ground. Just as with the Civil Rights Movement, they offer support and training for activists in an effort to maximize their effectiveness. The movement is a coalition of forces aimed at bringing about social change. In the same way that the Big Six civil rights leaders, which included Martin Luther King Jr., James Farmer, and A. Philip Randolph, were national spokespeople for the movement, so are figures like Alicia Garza, Patrisse Cullors, and Opal Tometi. Leadership is an area where Black Lives Matter tries to distinguish itself from the Civil Rights Movement, as Alicia Garza explained in an interview for The Guardian: "If you're only looking

> African Americans are incarcerated at more than five times the rate of White Americans

"POLICE ARE EVER-PRESENT IN BLACK COMMUNITIES"

Students from New York City schools at the second annual Future of the City March against police brutality

BLM co-founder Alicia Garza speaking at CitizenUCon16 in March 2016

BLM co-founder Opal Tometi on *The Laura Saunders Show* in August 2015

A march through Park Lane, London, in 2016, to demonstrate against the killing of Black men by police in the US

BLACK LIVES MATTER IN THE UK

One of the notable differences to the Civil Rights Movement is how BLM has spread across the world. The movement has inspired protests in countries such as France and South Africa, as well as becoming a driving force behind Black struggle in the UK. In July 2016, following the killings of Alton Sterling and Philando Castile, who was live-streamed bleeding out on Facebook, protests erupted across the UK. Thousands of mainly young people took to the streets in all the major cities protesting in solidarity. BLM UK had been organizing before, with the support of the American founders, but the movement gained national attention with these protests. In August 2016, BLM organized civil disobedience, shutting down the tram service in Nottingham, and blocking roads in Birmingham as well as the M4 exit to Heathrow Airport. BLM UK aims to raise the profile of those who have died in custody, or after police contact, in Britain, including Kingsley Burrell, Sarah Reed, Mzee Mohammed, and Mark Duggan. Just as in America, Black people in the UK are more likely to die under suspicious circumstances after police contact and are actually even more over-represented in the prison population. BLM UK has also broadened the issue from criminal justice to issues such as immigration, poverty, and climate justice.

"BLACK LIVES MATTER AIMS TO BE LEADERLESS IN ORDER TO PROMOTE A DIVERSITY OF VOICES"

for the straight Black man who is a preacher, you're not going to find it."

An enduring criticism of the civil rights struggle is that it was sexist and focused too narrowly on issues that impacted directly on men. We remember the charismatic male leaders who rallied the troops and set the agenda, and ignore the women who toiled behind the scenes. BLM has rejected this patriarchal idea, started by three gay Black women, it has aimed to empower a leaderful organization that is open to the whole Black community. Bayard Rustin is one of the most important civil rights activists but because he was gay, his story is most often overlooked. In contrast, DeRay Mckesson has become one of the most prominent voices associated with BLM. This is no small difference; civil rights was blighted by its pursuit of presenting a respectable version of blackness that would be palatable to mainstream America. Mckesson's mantra "I love my blackness, and yours" is the perfect response to the limits of past movements.

BLM aims to be leaderless in order to promote a diversity of voices but also to prevent damage caused by the figurehead being brought down or betraying the cause. Assassinations of figures like Martin

There have been more than 2,322 Black Lives Matter protests across the globe

Luther King Jr. act as a cautionary tale for investing too much in a leader. Emphasis is placed on being 'leaderful' and empowering activists within different chapters. This is more similar to the organizing of the Civil Rights Movement than we have been taught to remember. The figureheads may linger in the memory but the reality is that it was a broad coalition of Black activists that made the movement a success. BLM is actually more traditionally led, with a platform, chapters, and its own programs. In contrast, the Civil Rights Movement is a label we have placed over a range of different and sometimes competing ideas and organizations.

Trying to both lead, and be leaderless, puts BLM in a difficult practical position. In the desire to not dictate solutions, they have created BLM as more of a kitemark than an organization. A badge that sanctions the work of activists on the ground. When asked about the similarities between BLM and the Black Panther Party, former Panther Kathleen Cleaver insisted that they "were not a movement" but an organization. She stressed the clear ideology, structure, and programs of the Panthers, which is something that BLM purposefully lacks on the national level. The national agenda of BLM includes Channel Black, for media representation; a Black Futures Month program, and

BLM co-founder Patrisse Cullors accepting the Sydney Peace Prize in November 2017

DeRay Mckesson, a voice that has come to the fore in BLM

Colin Kaepernick (center) and teammates from the San Francisco 49ers take a knee in protest during the pre-game playing of the national anthem

COLIN KAEPERNICK STARTS NFL NATIONAL ANTHEM PROTESTS

In September 2016, San Francisco 49ers quarterback Colin Kaepernick brought international attention to the issue of police brutality and racism by refusing to stand for the national anthem, which is routinely played before every NFL game. He explained: "I am not going to stand up to show pride in a flag for a country that oppresses Black people and people of color." His protest was inspired by Black Lives Matter and before long, other players joined in by taking a knee during the anthem. The protests proved controversial with NFL owners, many fans, and even the US president. In October 2017, President Trump encouraged the NFL to take a zero-tolerance approach to players who "disrespect our flag, our country" and said that he would implore owners to say "get that son of a bitch off the field right now" if they refused to stand during the anthem. The following week over 200 NFL players took a knee. Since July 2017 Kaepernick has been without a team and is suing the NFL for collusion. He has continued his activism and donated $1 million to a range of social justice organizations.

a series of high-profile "provocateur events." This is a far cry from the Panthers' newspaper, free breakfast programs, medical clinics, legal advice, as well as strict party discipline being centrally administrated. It should not be a surprise that BLM is more similar to the Civil Rights Movement in terms of scope when the goals are similar: to protest in order to produce policy change. The Panthers could take up arms to defend the community from the police, while BLM engages in peaceful protest, because they were not interested in public opinion but revolutionary practice. Both groups gained a high profile by taking up the issues of criminal injustice, and the youth and urgency of BLM has created a connection to the Panthers in the popular imagination. But to really understand BLM we have to go back to a fissure that broke out within civil rights activists.

Younger and more militant activists in the Civil Rights Movement grew tired of the incremental, "overcome them with our capacity for love" approach of King and the leading organizations. Stokely Carmichael (later Kwame Ture), of the Student Nonviolent Coordinating Committee (SNCC) manifested

Defining moment

Trayvon Martin Feb 26, 2012

Neighborhood watch volunteer George Zimmerman fatally shoots unarmed 17-year-old Trayvon Martin as he returns from the shops in Sanford, Florida. Following the killing of Martin, rallies, marches, and protests take place across the United States. Claiming self-defense, Zimmerman isn't initially charged but increased attention from the media leads to him eventually being tried for Trayvon's murder. However, he is acquitted of second-degree murder and manslaughter in 2013. The killing of Trayvon and Zimmerman's acquittal is widely seen as the spark that led to the creation of the Black Lives Matter movement and its campaigns against violence and systemic racism towards Black people in America.

Timeline

2014

2012 **2013** **2014** **2014** **2014** **2015** **2015**

Miriam Carey, Washington, D.C.
While making a U-turn at a White House checkpoint, Carey hits a police car. Police give chase before shooting her dead. Her 13-month-old daughter is in the back of the car.
Oct 3, 2013

Laquan McDonald, Chicago
17-year-old McDonald is shot 16 times by a police officer. After a video of the incident is released, numerous protests are held across several months.
Oct 20, 2014

Tanisha Anderson, Cleveland
Anderson's family call 911 as she is having a mental-health episode. Police arrive and she dies as a result of being restrained on the ground by officers.
Nov 14, 2014

Tamir Rice, Cleveland
The 12-year-old is shot by a police officer as he plays with a toy gun. It is later revealed that the officer was deemed unfit for duty by his previous force.
Nov 22, 2014

Walter Scott, North Charleston
Unarmed, Scott is shot in the back as he attempts to flee from police. The officer claims Scott took his taser but an eyewitness video reveals this not to be true.
April 4, 2015

Freddie Gray, Baltimore
Gray fell into a coma shortly after being arrested. He died a week later due to injuries to his spinal cord. Protests are held throughout the country. **April 19, 2015**

A police officer patrols during a protest in support of BLM in New York on July 9, 2016

Ferguson has faced many protests since the shooting of Michael Brown by a police officer

this frustration when he used the term 'Black Power' at a rally in Mississippi in 1966. Black Power was a cry for recognition, to not have to accommodate the interests of White society in order for legislative change. Black Power is often seen as its own distinct movement, a rebuke to the more traditional civil rights leaders. We think of slogans like "Black is beautiful," the militancy of the Panthers, and Malcolm X's fiery speeches against the "White devils." In doing this we forget that the roots of Black Power were the Civil Rights Movement, young people frustrated by the slowness of change and tone of the struggle.

If social media were around in the 1960s, Black Power would have been a hashtag, a way to capture a range of ideas and feelings and to insist that Black life matters. When Malcolm X talked about the need to "elevate the civil rights struggle to the level of human rights," what he meant was that Black people were not respected as human beings. The phrase 'Black Lives Matter' is the simplest representation of that idea. You cannot legislate our basic recognition as people, and this is where BLM directly

"THERE IS THE FEELING IT IS TIME FOR A FRESH, GRASSROOTS APPROACH TO THE PROBLEMS"

embraces the legacy of Black Power and explains the generational divide between BLM and the surviving civil rights royalty.

Open hostility has been displayed towards some of the veterans of the Civil Rights Movement when they have tried to engage in the moment defined by BLM. At a rally in Washington in 2014, organized by Al Sharpton's organization, BLM activist Johnetta Elzie stormed the stage, upset that the younger activists' work was being co-opted. There is the feeling it is time for a fresh, grassroots approach to the problems and the established way of parachuting figureheads into hotspots has run its course. This split is not new and goes back to the debate in the 1960s. The younger activists were inspired by Malcolm X's urgency and bought into being Black Power, but it largely remained in the sphere of civil rights. There are a few examples who took up the revolutionary mantle, but in the main the

African Americans are almost three times more likely to be killed by the police than White people

movement aimed to better integrate African Americans into the system. Even cultural activists like Amiri Baraka, who wanted to maintain distinct African-American cultural communities, did so in tandem with civil rights gains. Baraka started a Committee For a Unified Newark (CFUN) in 1968, an organization that worked with Newark officials to try to carve out some space in the city for African Americans. This meant supporting electoral candidates and encouraging people to vote, rather than destroying the system.

Black Power became so loosely defined that it was used in calls for better integration into capitalism, as well as by those wanting to bring about communism. Black Lives Matter faces the same problem of being too broad a platform. It is almost as impossible to disagree that Black life matters, as it is to agree to what the solution is. In taking the coalition for policy reform model, BLM is the 21st century version of the Civil Rights Movement. The question now is whether we need to reinvent the civil rights approach, or abandon its politics for a more radical vision of revolution.

Defining moment

Eric Garner July 17, 2014
Garner is approached by police in New York on the belief that he was illegally selling cigarettes. One officer grabs Garner from behind before putting him in a chokehold or headlock for up to 20 seconds before he loses consciousness. In a video of the incident Garner can be seen yelling "I can't breathe" 11 times. He's pronounced dead at the hospital around an hour later. Garner's cause of death is ruled as compression of the neck. However, on December 3 a grand jury decides not to indict the officer responsible. By the end of the year around 50 protests against police brutality are held across the country.

HANDS UP DONT SHOOT AUG 9, 2014 R.I.P. MICHAEL BROWN

Defining moment

Michael Brown August 9, 2014
A police officer notices Brown fitting the description of a man who reportedly stole cigars from a store close to where they were in Ferguson, Missouri. The officer pulls his car next to Brown. After an altercation the officer shoots an unarmed Brown 12 times, killing him. Peaceful protests are held the day of the shooting but they soon turn violent, starting what is known as the Ferguson Unrest, with the slogan 'Hands Up, Don't Shoot' being widely chanted at demonstrations. No charges were filed against the officer. The killings of Martin, Garner, and Brown spark debate across America about the relationship between the police and Black Americans, fuelling the Black Lives Matter movement and bringing the issue of violence towards Black people into the eyes of the world.

2015
● Sandra Bland, Waller County
Bland is found hanged in a jail cell three days after being arrested during a traffic stop. Protesters call for an investigation into the cause of her death.
July 13, 2015

2016
● Alton Sterling, Baton Rouge
Sterling is shot several times while being held on the ground by two police officers. No charges are filed against the officers involved. **July 5, 2016**

2016
● Philando Castile, Falcon Heights
Seconds after Castile is shot by police, his girlfriend Diamond Reynolds livestreams a video to Facebook of the officers as Castile lays fatally wounded.
July 6, 2016

2016
● Korryn Gaines, Randallstown
Gaines is shot dead and her five-year-old son wounded during a standoff with police. Gaines records the incident, but Facebook deactivates her account due to a police request.
Aug 1, 2016

2020
● Breonna Taylor, Louisville
Police officers force entry into Taylor's apartment and shoot her six times, killing her. The officers are cleared of all charges, leading to protests across the US.
Mar 13, 2020

2020
● George Floyd, Minneapolis
Floyd is killed after police officer Derek Chauvin kneels on his neck for over nine minutes. Chauvin is convicted of his murder in 2021.
May 25, 2020

THE GEORGE FLOYD PROTESTS

George Floyd's brutal murder at the hands of police in Minneapolis in May 2020 sparked the largest protests in US history and spread around the globe

n early summer 2020, millions of protesters chanted "say his name" and "I can't breathe" as they called for the end of racism against Black people, prompted by the killing of George Floyd, a 46-year-old Black man. On May 25, 2020, he was murdered during an arrest in which Minneapolis police officer Derek Chauvin knelt on his neck for more than nine minutes, while three other officers prevented passers-by from intervening.

The George Floyd protests began just hours after the murder as a bystander's video was widely circulated on social media, in which Floyd is heard repeatedly saying "I can't breathe." Protesters started at the location of Floyd's arrest and murder in Minneapolis and took over the rest of the streets in the city. The Black Lives Matter (BLM) protests quickly spread nationwide to over 200 cities and towns, with polls estimating that between 15 and 26 million people had participated in demonstrations, making it the largest protest in US history. After receiving global media attention, the movement spread around the world. In over 60 different countries, protesters united to show their support for BLM. While most of the protests were peaceful, there were also violent clashes with the police.

A few days after Floyd's murder, former US president Donald Trump took to Twitter, calling the protesters "thugs" and writing: "When the looting starts, the shooting starts." Although it was later hidden by Twitter for 'glorifying violence', it's a phrase that has historically been used against Black protesters, not a statement of reconciliation.

The impact of the BLM protests is still to be determined. The protests made it clear that police departments had to make significant changes, so Congressional Democrats drafted an extensive police misconduct reform bill, called the George Floyd Justice in Policing Act, which sought to demilitarize the police and prevent police brutality. While the Democrat-controlled House approved it, the then-Republican-controlled Senate didn't. In the meantime, the Minneapolis Police Department has been forced by its city council to ban chokeholds and neck restraints, and 'no-knock warrants' are now banned in Louisville.

Another result of the protests is the removal or renaming of public monuments and street names. Nearly 170 statues, street names, and other tributes to the Confederacy have been removed or renamed in the US. However, there is still a long way to go to achieve racial justice and equality in the country.

Floyd's daughter (left) was left behind when her father was murdered by police

'Black Lives Matter' was painted on 16th St. in Washington, D.C., during the protests in summer 2020

Harris made history as the first ever Black female vice president of the United States

OFFICE of
**PRESIDENT
ELECT**

KAMALA HARRIS: FIRST BLACK, FEMALE VP

Inspired by Shirley Chisholm, in 2021 Kamala Harris broke new ground after becoming Joe Biden's vice president

The official portrait of Vice President Kamala Harris taken on March 5, 2021

Oakland, California, native Kamala Devi Harris was born to Shyamala Gopalan, who emigrated from India, and Jamaican Donald J. Harris. Inspired by her activist parents, Harris graduated from Howard University and the University of California. A sense of justice erupted from family participation in civil rights demonstrations and introductions to role models such as Supreme Court Justice Thurgood Marshall and civil rights leader Constance Baker Motley.

Harris became district attorney of San Francisco in 2003 and California's attorney general in 2010. In 2014, she married lawyer and future second gentleman Douglas Emhoff. They have a blended family including children Ella and Cole. Harris was sworn in as a United States senator in 2017.

Just three years later, Harris paid tribute to Shirley Chisholm's 1972 presidential campaign using similar colors and typography in her bid for the US presidency. The red-and-yellow design could be seen in a January 21, 2019 video announcement of Harris's run for the top job. In fact, Harris even launched her presidential campaign 47 years to the day after Chisholm's. However, she dropped out of the race not even 11 days later on December 3, 2019.

On August 11, 2020, however, Harris accepted Joe Biden's invitation to become his running mate. It was an all-round good decision: after their victory she became the first woman, the first Black American, and the first South Asian American to be elected vice president of the United States of America in 2021. She is, however, determined not to be the last. Harris wore a purple dress in Shirley Chisholm's honor during her inauguration as she stepped out to Mary J Blige's *Work It*.

Though not unusual for a vice president, Harris has faced some criticism and negative press, particularly for her stance on border issues and immigration. She subsequently seemed to lag in popularity behind President Biden, with her poll numbers causing some concern. She was rarely seen in public in 2021, but her accomplishments continue to give hope to a generation of young girls worldwide.